HIGH PROTEIN
HIGH FIBER

MEAL PREP COOKBOOK

The Ultimate Guide to Fueling Your Body, Losing Weight, and Feeling Great with Nutrient-Dense Meals including a 30 day meal plan

GRACE K. WHITMORE

TABLE OF CONTENTS

INTRODUCTION

In today's fast-paced society, where many individuals strive for greater health and fitness, two dietary components—protein and fiber—are particularly beneficial. Incorporating high-protein and high-fiber foods into your daily diet will improve your general health, weight control, and long-term well-being. Let's look at the separate benefits of a high-protein diet, the significance of fiber, and how combining them results in a powerful synergy for optimal health.

In the pages ahead, I'll guide you through the science of inflammation and its connection to the foods we eat. You'll discover which foods have powerful anti-inflammatory properties and how to build a balanced diet around them. I'll also outline which foods to avoid, especially those that can fuel chronic inflammation. Whether you're new to meal planning or a seasoned home cook, this book provides easy, accessible recipes and practical strategies to incorporate these nourishing foods into your daily routine.

This book is crafted to be your comprehensive guide, complete with a 30-day meal plan to kick-start your journey toward better health. It's designed to be beginner-friendly, offering simple instructions and easy-to-find ingredients that make eating for your health both enjoyable and achievable. Whether you're looking to manage a chronic condition, improve your energy levels, or simply adopt a healthier way of eating, this book will empower you to take control of your diet and, in turn, your long-term health.

Advantages of a High-Protein Diet

The body requires protein for a variety of tasks, including muscle repair and immunological response. Its importance in metabolism, hunger regulation, and energy balance makes it essential for anyone wanting to lose weight, gain muscle, or simply live a healthy lifestyle.

1. Weight Loss: A high-protein diet aids in weight loss by boosting thermogenesis, a process in which your body burns more calories while digesting. Protein has a larger thermic impact than fats and carbs, so your body expends more energy to digest it. Furthermore, protein-rich foods promote sensations of fullness, allowing you to cut your overall calorie consumption without feeling deprived. This hunger control makes it easier to maintain a calorie deficit, which is required for weight loss.

2. Muscle Building and Maintenance: Protein is the fundamental structural component of muscle tissue. Resistance training or any other sort of physical activity causes small rips in your muscles. Consuming enough protein helps to repair and rebuild these muscles, resulting in greater strength and muscle mass over time. Even if you're not a bodybuilder or an athlete, maintaining lean muscle mass is vital for metabolism and overall physical function, especially as we get older.

3. Satiety and reduced cravings: Protein helps regulate hunger hormones such as ghrelin and leptin. Protein keeps you satiated for longer, which minimizes the need to snack between meals or go for high-calorie, processed foods. This is very useful for weight management and blood sugar control. According to studies, high-protein meals can reduce cravings for harmful foods while also encouraging more attentive eating behaviors.

Fiber is important for digestive health, blood sugar control, and overall well-being.

While protein receives a lot of attention in the nutrition industry, fiber is just as important for keeping a healthy body. Plant-based meals contain fiber, which is an indigestible carbohydrate that travels through the digestive system and delivers a number of health advantages.

1. Digestive health: Fiber is needed for proper digestion. It bulks up the stool and makes it pass more readily through the digestive tract, avoiding constipation and encouraging regular bowel motions. Soluble fiber, in particular, serves to feed beneficial bacteria in the gut, promoting a healthy microbiome and improving digestion and immunological function. A healthy gut can also help avoid digestive problems like IBS and diverticulitis.

2. Blood Sugar Control: Fiber slows sugar absorption in the bloodstream, reducing rapid rises in blood glucose levels. This is especially essential for people with diabetes or prediabetes because a high-fiber diet can help keep blood sugar levels steady and lower the likelihood of insulin resistance. Foods high in fiber, particularly soluble fiber (found in oats, beans, and certain fruits), produce a gel-like material in the gut, slowing the rate of sugar absorption into the blood.

3. Overall Wellbeing: Fiber has been linked to a variety of long-term health benefits, including a lower risk of heart disease, certain malignancies, and high cholesterol. It aids in the removal of excess cholesterol from the body by attaching to it in the digestive system and transporting it out via feces. Furthermore, fiber-rich foods are generally nutrient-dense, low in calories, and help promote a more balanced and sustainable diet.

Synergistic Effects: Combining High Protein with High Fiber in a Balanced Diet

While protein and fiber have significant health benefits on their own, combining high-both protein and high-fiber diets can enhance these effects for maximum health.

1. Improved satisfaction and appetite control: Protein and fiber work together to increase meal satisfaction by targeting both short- and long-term hunger triggers. Protein reduces immediate hunger by influencing hunger hormones, whereas fiber encourages a slow, continuous release of energy, keeping you full for extended periods of time. This synergy minimizes overeating and makes weight management more achievable.

2. Improved Blood Sugar Regulation: Combining fiber and protein can improve blood sugar control compared to consuming either macronutrient alone. For example, pairing high-protein foods like lean meats, eggs, or legumes with fiber-rich foods like whole grains or vegetables slows carbohydrate digestion. This reduces blood sugar spikes, making it an excellent method for treating diabetes and preventing insulin resistance.

3. Support for muscle and digestive health: High-protein, high-fiber diets make an effective combination for preserving muscle mass and boosting digestive health. For example, legumes such as lentils, chickpeas, and black beans are high in protein and fiber, making them an ideal dietary choice for people aiming to build or maintain muscle while also supporting gastrointestinal health.

4. Long-term cardiovascular health and disease prevention: A diet rich in protein and fiber has been linked to a lower risk of cardiovascular disease. Protein promotes muscle and tissue regeneration, whereas fiber lowers cholesterol and blood sugar levels, both of which are risk factors for heart disease. Additionally, fiber aids with weight management, which contributes to overall heart health.

Advantages of Weight Loss, Gut Health, and Energy

In the pursuit of better health and well-being, a diet high in protein and fiber has proven to be an effective tool. Whether you want to lose weight, enhance intestinal health, or have more energy throughout the day, concentrating on these two critical nutrients can make a big difference. Here's a closer look at how a high-protein, high-fiber diet promotes these three key characteristics of a healthy lifestyle.

1. Weight Loss: How High Protein and Fiber Can Help You Reach Your Goals

One of the most efficient ways to reduce weight is to follow a high-protein, high-fiber diet. These two macronutrients act together to regulate appetite, boost metabolism, and lower overall calorie intake.

- Protein for Satiety and Muscle Preservation: Protein has been shown to enhance satiety, or the sense of being full after eating, which is important for appetite management. Protein reduces cravings and the desire to snack between meals by modulating hunger hormones such as ghrelin and leptin. This makes it simple to follow a calorie-controlled diet without feeling restricted. Furthermore, protein helps to maintain lean muscle mass during weight loss, which is significant because muscle burns more calories at rest than fat. This increases metabolism, making weight loss more effective.
- Fiber to Control Appetite and Reduce Calories: Fiber adds weight to foods without increasing calories. Soluble fiber, in instance, forms a gel-like material in the stomach, slowing digestion and keeping you full for longer. This prolonged digestion prevents rapid reductions in blood sugar, which can cause energy dumps and cravings for sugary or high-calorie foods. Fiber promotes feelings of fullness, which helps lower overall calorie consumption, resulting in moderate, long-term weight loss.
- How Protein and Fiber Work Together to Help You Lose Weight: Protein and fiber work together to form an effective weight-management combo. Protein reduces appetite via influencing short-term hunger cues, whereas fiber increases fullness by slowing digestion. This dual strategy makes it easier to limit portion sizes, avoid overeating, and stick to a long-term weight loss plan.

2. Gut health: the role of fiber in preventing digestive issues.

Maintaining gut health is critical for general well-being, and fiber is an essential component for a healthy digestive tract. It not only promotes regular bowel movements but also helps to maintain a healthy gut microbiota and prevent digestive problems.

- Promoting regular bowel movements: Whole grains, vegetables, and seeds include insoluble fiber, which bulks out the stool and allows it to travel more readily through the digestive tract. This reduces constipation and encourages regular bowel movements, lowering the risk of gastrointestinal problems such as diverticulosis and hemorrhoids.
- Feeding your gut microbiome: Soluble fiber, found in foods such as oats, lentils, and fruits, provides nourishment for the healthy bacteria in your stomach. These bacteria convert fiber to short-chain fatty acids (SCFAs), which are anti-inflammatory and beneficial to gut health. A healthy microbiome has been linked to enhanced digestion, immunity, and even mental health.

- Preventing Digestive Disorders A fiber-rich diet can help prevent or treat common digestive problems like irritable bowel syndrome (IBS) and inflammatory bowel disease (IBD). Fiber-rich meals promote regularity and reduce inflammation in the gut, helping to maintain overall digestive system function, which is critical for nutrient absorption and long-term health.

3. Energy: How a Balanced Diet Maintains Energy Levels

Maintaining continuous energy throughout the day is critical to productivity and well-being. A balanced diet that contains both high-protein and high-fiber meals keeps your energy levels stable, preventing the highs and lows that come with unhealthy eating habits.

- Protein for Consistent Energy and Muscle Maintenance: Protein helps to stabilize blood sugar levels, providing a continuous amount of energy throughout the day. Unlike simple carbs, which can cause abrupt spikes and decreases in energy, protein releases energy gradually. This is especially crucial for physically demanding activities that require muscle strength and endurance. Protein also aids in muscle repair and regeneration after exercise, keeping your body invigorated and robust.
- Fiber with Slow Energy Release: Fiber, particularly soluble fiber, influences how rapidly sugars are taken into the bloodstream. Fiber, by slowing carbohydrate digestion, prevents rapid rises in blood sugar followed by sudden reductions, which can cause weariness and low energy levels. This moderate, continuous release of energy helps you avoid the mid-afternoon energy collapse that is common after a meal high in processed carbs and sugar.
- Balanced Meals to Maintain Energy: A diet rich in protein and fiber helps keep blood sugar levels steady throughout the day, allowing you to stay energetic. For example, a meal that includes a lean protein such as chicken or fish, as well as fiber-rich vegetables and whole grains, offers a continuous release of energy and helps reduce feelings of sluggishness or hunger soon after eating. This balance also improves mental attention and concentration, making it simpler to maintain productivity.

A high-protein, high-fiber diet is an effective way to lose weight, improve intestinal health, and keep energy levels steady throughout the day. Protein promotes satiety, muscle preservation, and sustained energy, whereas fiber improves digestive health, controls blood sugar, and promotes fullness. Together, these two nutrients offer a balanced and sustainable approach to achieving your health and wellness objectives, making it easier to feel your best every day. Incorporating additional high-protein and high-fiber foods into your daily routine can have long-term benefits for your weight, gut, and energy.

How To Use This Cookbook

Welcome to a gourmet journey that will encourage healthier eating habits, increase your energy, and simplify meal preparation! This cookbook is designed to help you include high-protein, high-fiber foods into your daily routine, making it simpler to meet your weight reduction, gut health, and energy goals. Whether you're a beginner or an expert home chef, this guide will help you maximize each dish and meal plan in the cookbook.

Structure and Content of the Cookbook

This cookbook is designed to provide a diverse collection of recipes, advice, and tools to meet a variety of dietary needs, schedules, and preferences. Here's an overview of what you'll discover:

1. Recipe Sections:
The recipes are organized into various categories, making it simple for you to navigate based on your needs:

Breakfasts: Energizing, nutrient-dense meals to help you start the day well.
Lunches: Delicious noon dishes that are simple to make and ideal for meal planning.
Dinners: Tasty and filling main courses that balance protein and fiber for good health.
Snacks and Sides: Quick, healthful options to satisfy hunger in between meals.
Smoothies and Drinks: Protein-rich smoothies and beverages to keep you energized and satisfied.
Desserts: sweets with a healthful twist, allowing you to indulge without guilt.

2. Meal plans:
In addition to individual recipes, this cookbook has pre-planned weekly menus. These meal plans simplify meal planning and are intended to save you time while keeping you on track with your health goals. Each plan strikes a balance between protein and fiber to promote long-term energy, weight management, and digestive health.

Guidelines for Using the Recipes and Meal Plans

These tips will help you use this cookbook's recipes and meal plans:

1. Begin Simple: If you're new to high-protein or high-fiber meals, start with basic recipes that require fewer ingredients and less preparation time. This will boost your confidence in the kitchen while also providing health benefits. Breakfasts and snacks are ideal beginning points because they are simple to include in a hectic schedule.
2. Follow these meal plans (or create your own): The meal plans are intended to provide a balanced intake of protein, fiber, and other vital nutrients. If you prefer a more structured approach, stick to the programs as written and use the grocery lists given. Alternatively, you can mix and match recipes to suit your taste or timetable. You can construct your own weekly menu by picking dishes from various areas, ensuring that protein and fiber are balanced.

3. Portion Control: Pay close attention to the recommended serving quantities, particularly if you have specific weight loss or muscle-building goals. Protein and fiber both help you feel full, so the dishes are intended to be satisfying without requiring big servings. If you're meal preparing, consider doubling or splitting recipes based on the number of servings you need.

4. Meal preparation and batch cooking:

Many recipes are designed to be meal-prep friendly, allowing you to create larger batches and freeze them for later in the week. This is very great for quick lunches and supper. Batch cooking on weekends might also help you save time throughout the busy week.

5. Ingredient Substitutions and Alternatives: Each recipe includes ideas for ingredient alternatives based on dietary choices, allergies, or product availability. This cookbook offers plenty of options, whether you're gluten-free, vegetarian, or simply working with what you have in the cupboard. For example, if a dish asks for chicken, you may replace it with tofu or tempeh to make a vegan alternative.

Adapting and Customizing Recipes to Your Preferences

While this cookbook includes a wide variety of recipes, it is also intended to inspire personalization. Feel free to alter and change the recipes to fit your personal preferences, dietary requirements, and lifestyle.

1. Adjusting seasonings and flavors: Everyone's taste buds are unique, so don't be afraid to experiment with different seasoning combinations. If you want strong flavors, add extra herbs and spices, or reduce the amount for a milder taste. Experiment with diverse taste profiles, such as Mediterranean, Asian, or Latin-inspired ingredients, to make your meals feel new and intriguing.

2. Switching Up Protein and Fiber Sources: The protein and fiber sources in the dishes are diverse. For example, you can replace chicken with turkey, beef, or a plant-based protein such as beans, lentils, or tempeh. Similarly, feel free to vary your fiber sources—try quinoa instead of brown rice, or replace leafy greens with cruciferous vegetables like broccoli or cauliflower.

3. Tailoring recipes to dietary preferences If you follow a certain diet, such as keto, paleo, or vegan, most recipes can be modified to meet your needs. For example, many high-protein meals can be keto-friendly by replacing starchy vegetables or grains with low-carb alternatives. Similarly, you can simply produce plant-based versions of most cuisines by replacing animal proteins with legumes, nuts, or seeds.

4. Scaling Recipes to Different Serving Sizes: Many recipes can be scaled up or down to serve a single person or a family. Look for the "Make It Your Way" instructions in the recipes to help you change ingredient quantities and cooking times to meet your specific needs.

5. Adding Extra Nutrients: Don't be afraid to add extra nutrients to your meals by including more vegetables, nuts, seeds, or healthy fats. For an added burst of fiber, vitamins, and healthy fats, try adding a handful of spinach or kale to a smoothie, chia seeds to your salad, or avocado to a protein-packed sandwich.

This cookbook is intended to be a versatile, user-friendly resource for preparing well-balanced, nutritious meals. While the recipes serve as a good foundation, you are invited to modify them based on your taste preferences and health goals. This cookbook can help you lose weight, enhance your intestinal health, and maintain consistent energy levels. Enjoy experimenting, adjusting, and making meals that your family will enjoy!

CHAPTER 1

Understanding Macronutrients

Protein, The Building Block

Proteins are the foundation of every cell, tissue, and organ in the body, earning them the nickname "building blocks of life." Whether you want to gain muscle, repair damaged tissues, or maintain overall health, protein plays an important part in almost every biological function. In this chapter, we will look at the importance of protein, the many types and sources, and the difference between complete and incomplete proteins to help you make informed dietary decisions.

Protein's Importance for Tissue Building and Repair

Protein is required to maintain, create, and repair the body's tissues. Proteins play an important role in muscle fiber repair, wound healing, and cell regeneration whenever we engage in physical activity, become ill, or suffer body stress. Aside from muscle repair, protein promotes the production and function of enzymes, hormones, and antibodies, all of which are essential for daily health.

- Muscle Development and Maintenance: Proteins are responsible for muscle synthesis, which is the process by which your body creates and repairs muscle tissues. Protein aids in muscle repair and growth following exercise, particularly strength training. Muscles cannot heal adequately without an adequate protein intake, which can result in weakness or even muscular disintegration.
- Tissue Repair: Proteins serve an important role in healing and tissue regeneration. When you are injured, protein helps to rebuild damaged tissues, promoting wound healing and recovery. Proteins also aid in the renewal of skin, organs, and blood cells, which helps the body function properly.
- Enzyme and Hormonal Support: Many enzymes and hormones in the body are made of proteins. These enzymes accelerate chemical activities in the body, ranging from digestion to energy production, whereas hormones such as insulin and glucagon regulate essential internal functions like metabolism and blood glucose levels.

Protein Types and Sources

Proteins can be obtained from a range of meals, both animal and plant-based. It's critical to recognize that not all proteins are created equal, and different sources offer diverse amino acid profiles and health benefits.

1. Animal-based proteins: Animal proteins are deemed high-quality because they include all of the essential amino acids that the body is incapable of producing on its own. Common sources include:
- Meat: chicken, beef, hog, and lamb.
- Fish and seafood (such as salmon, tuna, and shrimp)
- Eggs
- Dairy products (milk, cheese, and yogurt).

These proteins are "complete," which means they include the entire range of amino acids, making them optimal for muscle development and tissue repair. They are also highly bioavailable, which means that the body can readily absorb and use them.

2. Plant-Based Protein: Plant proteins are derived from beans, legumes, grains, nuts, and seeds. While plant-based proteins are frequently regarded as healthier due to their lower saturated fat and cholesterol content, they may be deficient in amino acids. Typical plant protein sources include:
- Legumes (lentils, chickpeas, and black beans)
- Quinoa (an unusual plant-based full protein)
- Nuts and seeds, including almonds, chia seeds, and hemp seeds.
- Tofu and tempeh.
- Whole grains (brown rice and oats)

Although some plant-based proteins are incomplete, combining several plant-based sources (such as rice and beans) can offer all of the necessary amino acids, resulting in a complete protein.

3. Protein supplements: Protein powders and supplements are useful for those wishing to quickly increase their protein consumption, particularly after exercise. There are various kinds of protein supplements:
- Whey Protein: A complete, quick-digesting animal protein that is great for post-workout recovery.
- Casein Protein: A slow-digesting milk protein that promotes muscle regeneration over time, particularly during sleep.
- Plant-Based Protein Powders: These alternatives, derived from sources such as pea, soy, or rice protein, are suitable for vegetarians and vegans; however, they may need to be blended with other sources to get a complete amino acid profile.

Difference between complete and incomplete proteins?

Understanding the distinction between complete and incomplete proteins can help you improve your nutrition for certain health objectives, such as muscle gain, weight loss, or overall well-being

1. Complete proteins: A complete protein includes all nine essential amino acids, which the body cannot create on its own. These essential amino acids are required for muscle development, tissue repair, and a variety of metabolic functions. Complete proteins are commonly present in animal-based meals such as meat, poultry, fish, eggs, and dairy products. However, there are certain plant-based complete proteins, such as quinoa, buckwheat, and soy.

Benefits of Complete Proteins:

Optimal Muscle Repair: Complete proteins contain all of the essential amino acids, making them perfect for athletes or anybody interested in muscle growth and repair.

Efficient Tissue Healing: Having a complete set of amino acids allows the body to properly repair tissue and regenerate cells.

Easy Digestibility: Animal-based complete proteins are more bioavailable, which means the body can break them down and absorb them more effectively.

2. Incomplete proteins: Incomplete proteins lack one or more necessary amino acids. The majority of plant-based proteins fall into this group, with the exception of quinoa and soy. However, joining partial proteins can result in a complete amino acid profile. For example, combining rice and beans results in a complete protein source.

Benefits of Incomplete Proteins

Lower in Saturated Fat: Plant-based proteins often contain fewer harmful fats, which can be good for heart health.

High in fiber and antioxidants: Many plant protein sources are high in fiber, vitamins, and antioxidants, which help improve digestive health and reduce the risk of chronic diseases.

Sustainability: Plant-based protein sources have a lesser environmental impact than animal-based proteins, making them a more sustainable diet option.

Fiber, the Unsung Hero

While protein is frequently the focus of nutrition conversations, fiber is an equally important—and sometimes overlooked—component of a healthy diet. Fiber helps to preserve digestive health, regulate blood sugar, decrease cholesterol, and promote general well-being. In this chapter, we'll examine fiber types, origins, and health benefits.

Fiber Types and Sources

Fiber is a carbohydrates that the body cannot completely digest. It typically passes through the digestive system unharmed, offering a number of health benefits in the process. Fiber is classified into two types: soluble and insoluble, with each having its own set of qualities and health benefits.

1. Soluble Fiber: Soluble fiber dissolves in water, resulting in a gel-like substance in the digestive tract. This gel slows digestion, which helps regulate blood sugar and cholesterol levels. It also promotes a sense of fullness, which can benefit with weight management.

Common sources of soluble fiber:
- Oats
- Barley
- Beans and legumes.
- Apples, oranges, and other citrus fruits.
- Carrots
- Psyllium Husk.
- Flaxseeds

2. Insoluble Fibers: Insoluble fiber does not dissolve in water and adds weight to the stool, allowing food to move more swiftly through the stomach and intestines. This form of fiber encourages regular bowel movements and reduces constipation, improving overall digestive health.

Common sources of insoluble fiber:
- Whole grains (wheat, brown rice, and quinoa).
- Vegetables, particularly leafy greens, cauliflower, and root vegetables.
- Nuts and seeds.
- wheat bran.
- Potatoes with skin

Many plant-based foods have both forms of fiber, so incorporating a variety of fruits, vegetables, whole grains, legumes, and nuts into your diet will provide a healthy balance of soluble and insoluble fiber.

The Advantages of Soluble and Insoluble Fiber for Digestive Health and Well-Being

Fiber is needed for a healthy digestive tract and a variety of other body processes. Let's look at how soluble and insoluble fiber benefit digestive health and beyond.

1. Soluble Fiber Promotes Gut Health and Satiety: Improves Digestion: Soluble fiber feeds the good bacteria in your gut, helping to maintain a healthy gut microbiota. These bacteria convert fiber into short-chain fatty acids (SCFAs), which reduce inflammation and improve the gut lining.

- Increases Fullness: The gel generated by soluble fiber slows digestion, allowing you to feel fuller for longer after eating. This can help with overall calorie consumption and weight management.
- Reduces Digestive Discomfort: Soluble fiber can help control irritable bowel syndrome (IBS) by softening stools and preventing diarrhea.

2. Insoluble fiber promotes colon health and regularity.

- Prevents constipation: Insoluble fiber bulks up the stool, making it easier to move through the intestines. This encourages regular bowel motions and prevents digestive problems such as constipation, hemorrhoids, and diverticulosis.

Meal Planning and Preparation Strategies for Beginners

Effective meal planning and preparation can greatly simplify your path to adopting an anti-inflammatory diet. This section gives practical tips for constructing a weekly meal plan, covers the advantages of batch cooking and meal preparation, and advises on safe food storage to ensure freshness.

Tips for Making a Weekly Meal Plan

1. Set aside time for planning: Set dedicate a dedicated day each week to arrange your meals. This may be Sunday afternoon or any other day that fits into your calendar. Take advantage of this opportunity to see what ingredients you have on hand and what you'll need for the coming week.
2. Choose a variety of foods: Include a variety of fruits, vegetables, whole grains, lean proteins, and healthy fats in your meal plan. This not only keeps meals interesting but also guarantees that you get a diverse range of nutrients.
3. Include meals and snacks. Plan for breakfast, lunch, dinner, and snacks. Consider quick snack options like cut-up vegetables, nuts, or yogurt to keep you full between meals and avoid reaching for less nutritious options.
4. Select Simple Recipes: Choose recipes that require minimal materials. Look for dishes using comparable components to cut waste and simplify grocery shopping.

5. Plan for Leftovers: Include meals that will result in leftovers. For example, roast a greater quantity of veggies or protein that may be utilized in a variety of dishes throughout the week.

6. Make a grocery list: Once your meal plan is finalized, make a comprehensive grocery list based on the ingredients you'll require. To make shopping more effective, organize the list into categories (fruit, dairy, grains, etc.).

7. Allow for flexibility in your meal plan to accommodate life's unexpected events. If your plans change, keep quick, nutritious dinner options on hand to prevent making last-minute harmful choices.

Benefits of Batch Cooking and Meal Preparation

1. Time-saving: Batch cooking reduces weekly cooking time by preparing numerous meals at once. This is very useful for busy people or families.

2. Stay Consistent with Dietary Goals: Preparing meals ahead of time makes it easier to keep to anti-inflammatory diet concepts and avoid processed foods.

3. Cost-Effective: Purchasing materials in bulk and cooking in batches helps reduce costs. It reduces the number of trips to the grocery shop and food waste.

4. Stress reduction: Having prepared meals relieves the stress of deciding what to cook each day. You may simply reheat a meal or assemble a quick dish without the stress of starting from scratch.

5. Promotes healthier choices: When you have nutritious meals and snacks on hand, you are less likely to cave to cravings for harmful or convenient items.

Guidelines for Proper Food Storage

1. Use Airtight Containers: Purchase high-quality airtight containers to store prepared meals, leftovers, and fresh produce. These containers help to preserve freshness and avoid spoiling.

2. Label and Date: Label containers with contents and date of preparation. This technique allows you to maintain track of freshness and easily find what you need in the fridge or freezer.

3. Organize the Fridge: Keep prepared meals at eye level for easy access. Keep frequently used items near the front, and eat leftovers within a few days.

4. Use the Freezer: Freeze parts of cooked meals or specific components, like grains or roasted veggies. This allows you to retain variety while reducing food waste. Ensure that things are properly labeled and stored in freezer-safe containers.

5. Store produce correctly: Fruits and vegetables have variable storage requirements. Leafy greens, for example, should be refrigerated in perforated bags, whereas root vegetables can be stored in a cool, dark spot. Always wash vegetables right before use to avoid moisture buildup, which can contribute to deterioration.

6. Regularly check expiration dates on packaged products and pantry items. Consume older items first to reduce waste.

7. Rotate Stock: Apply the "first in, first out" guideline while stocking your pantry or refrigerator. Place newer products below older ones to avoid forgetting and spoiling.

Chapter 2

~⌘~

HIGH PROTEIN HIGH FIBER RECIPES

BREAKFAST RECIPES

BERRY PROTEIN BLAST

PREP TIME

5 Minutes

COOK TIME

10 minutes

SERVING SIZE

2 servings

YIELD

......

NUTRITIONAL VALUE

- Calories: 250 Protein: 25g
- Fat: 8g Carbohydrates: 28g
- Fiber: 8g

INGREDIENT

- 1 cup mixed berries (fresh or frozen)
- 1 scoop vanilla protein powder
- 1/2 cup unsweetened almond milk
- 1/2 cup Greek yogurt
- 1 tablespoon chia seeds
- 1 tablespoon honey (optional)

INSTRUCTIONS

- 1. Place the mixed berries, protein powder, and almond milk into a blender.
- 2. Add the Greek yogurt for a creamy texture.
- 3. Sprinkle in the chia seeds for extra fiber and omega3s.
- 4. Blend on high until smooth, adjusting the consistency with additional almond milk if needed.
- 5. Taste and add honey if you prefer a sweeter smoothie.
- 6. Pour into a glass and enjoy immediately.

TIPS

To enhance the antiinflammatory benefits, be sure to add the black pepper, which helps your body absorb the curcumin in turmeric.

APPLE CINNAMON OVERNIGHT OATS

 PREP TIME
10 minutes

 CHILL TIME
4 hours (or overnight)

SERVING SIZE
2 servings

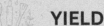 **YIELD**
......

NUTRITIONAL VALUE

- Calories: 320 | Protein: 7g
- Carbohydrates: 58g | Fat: 9g
- Fiber: 10g | Sugar: 18g

INGREDIENT

- 1 cup rolled oats
- 1 cup unsweetened almond milk (or milk of choice)
- 1/2 cup unsweetened applesauce
- 1/2 teaspoon ground cinnamon
- 1 tablespoon chia seeds
- 1 tablespoon maple syrup or honey
- 1/4 teaspoon vanilla extract
- 1 small apple, chopped
- 2 tablespoons chopped walnuts (optional for crunch)

TIPS

For a more indulgent flavor, you can substitute applesauce with grated fresh apples.
You can add protein powder or Greek yogurt to the mixture for an extra protein boost.

INSTRUCTIONS

- 1. In a mason jar or airtight container, combine the oats, almond milk, applesauce, cinnamon, chia seeds, maple syrup, and vanilla extract.
- 2. Stir well until all ingredients are fully combined.
- 3. Cover the container and refrigerate for at least 4 hours, or preferably overnight.
- 4. When ready to serve, stir the oats again to make sure they are wellmixed and creamy.
- 5. Chop the apple and stir half into the oats, reserving the other half for topping.
- 6. Divide the oats into two bowls, and top each with the remaining chopped apple and walnuts (if using).
- 7. Enjoy chilled or heat it up for a warm breakfast!

GREEN MACHINE

PREP TIME
10 minutes

CHILL TIME
0 minutes (blend and serve)

SERVING SIZE
2 servings

YIELD
......

NUTRITIONAL VALUE
- Calories: 320 | Protein: 9g
- Carbohydrates: 25g | Fat: 22g
- Fiber: 10g | Sugar: 8g

INGREDIENT

- 1 cup spinach or kale (fresh or frozen)
- 1/2 frozen banana
- 1/4 avocado
- 1/2 cup unsweetened almond milk (or coconut water)
- 1 tablespoon chia seeds
- 1 tablespoon almond butter
- 1/2 teaspoon ground turmeric
- 1/2 teaspoon ground ginger
- 1/4 teaspoon black pepper (to enhance turmeric absorption)

TOPPINGS:
- 1/4 cup sliced kiwi
- 1 tablespoon pumpkin seeds
- 1 teaspoon hemp seeds

TIPS
For a thicker, creamier texture, you can freeze the avocado ahead of time.
Substitute almond butter with any nut or seed butter if you have allergies.

INSTRUCTIONS

- 1. In a blender, combine spinach (or kale), frozen banana, avocado, almond milk, chia seeds, almond butter, turmeric, ginger, and black pepper.
- 2. Blend on high until smooth and creamy. You can add more almond milk if the mixture is too thick for your preference.
- 3. Pour the smoothie into a bowl, using a spoon to smooth out the top.
- 4. Arrange the toppings: layer sliced kiwi, sprinkle pumpkin seeds, shredded coconut, and hemp seeds for added texture and nutrition.
- 5. Serve immediately and enjoy the fresh, vibrant flavors.

CHOCOLATE PEANUT BUTTER CUP

PREP TIME
5 minutes

CHILL TIME
0 minutes (blend and serve)

SERVING SIZE
1 serving

YIELD
......

NUTRITIONAL VALUE
- Calories: 290 | Protein: 10g
- Carbohydrates: 38g | Fat: 12g
- Fiber: 12g | Sugar: 18g

INGREDIENT

- 1/2 cup frozen mixed berries (blueberries, raspberries, strawberries)
- 1/2 frozen banana
- 1/4 cup unsweetened almond milk
- 1/4 cup plain Greek yogurt (or a dairyfree alternative)
- 1 tablespoon ground flaxseeds
- 1 tablespoon chia seeds
- 1/2 teaspoon ground cinnamon
- 1 teaspoon honey or maple syrup (optional)

TIPS
You can use any combination of frozen berries you prefer for the base, and add more fresh berries on top for a burst of flavor.
Substitute Greek yogurt with a plantbased yogurt to make this recipe dairyfree.

INSTRUCTIONS

- 1. In a blender, combine frozen mixed berries, banana, almond milk, Greek yogurt, ground flaxseeds, chia seeds, cinnamon, and honey (if using).
- 2. Blend until smooth and thick. If you prefer a thinner consistency, add more almond milk a tablespoon at a time.
- 3. Pour the smoothie mixture into a bowl and spread evenly.
- 4. Top with fresh berries, granola (if using), and a sprinkle of chia seeds for added crunch and nutrients.
- 5. Serve immediately and enjoy this antioxidantpacked, antiinflammatory treat.

TOPPINGS

- 1/4 cup fresh berries (blueberries, raspberries)
- 1 tablespoon granola (optional for crunch)
- 1 teaspoon chia seeds

MEDITERRANEAN VEGETABLE FRITTATA

PREP TIME
10 minutes

CHILL TIME
20 minutes

SERVING SIZE
4 servings

YIELD
......

NUTRITIONAL VALUE
- Calories: 220 | Protein: 12g
- Carbohydrates: 6g | Fat: 16g
- Fiber: 2g | Sugar: 4g

INGREDIENT

- 6 large eggs
- 1/4 cup almond milk (or dairy milk)
- 1/2 cup cherry tomatoes, halved
- 1/2 cup zucchini, diced
- 1/4 cup red bell pepper, diced
- 1/4 cup red onion, diced
- 1/4 cup crumbled feta cheese
- 1 tablespoon olive oil
- 1 teaspoon dried oregano
- Salt and pepper to taste
- Fresh basil for garnish (optional)

TIPS

Make sure your skillet is ovensafe to avoid transferring the frittata to another dish. Cast iron works great for this recipe.
You can substitute any vegetables you prefer, such as spinach or eggplant, for a different variation

INSTRUCTIONS

- 1. Preheat the oven to 375°F (190°C).
- 2. In a medium bowl, whisk together the eggs, almond milk, oregano, salt, and pepper.
- 3. Heat the olive oil in an ovensafe skillet over medium heat. Add the red onion, zucchini, bell pepper, and cherry tomatoes, and sauté for 3–4 minutes, until slightly softened.
- 4. Pour the egg mixture into the skillet over the sautéed vegetables. Stir gently to ensure the vegetables are evenly distributed.
- 5. Sprinkle the crumbled feta cheese on top of the egg mixture.
- 6. Transfer the skillet to the preheated oven and bake for 15–20 minutes, or until the frittata is set in the center and golden on top.
- 7. Remove from the oven, garnish with fresh basil if desired, and serve warm.

SPINACH AND MUSHROOM EGG MUFFINS

 PREP TIME
10 minutes

 CHILL TIME
20 minutes

 SERVING SIZE
6 egg muffins

YIELD
......

NUTRITIONAL VALUE

- Calories: 120 | Protein: 8g
- Carbohydrates: 2g | Fat: 9g
- Fiber: 1g | Sugar: 1g

INGREDIENT

- 6 large eggs
- 1/4 cup unsweetened almond milk (or milk of choice)
- 1 cup fresh spinach, chopped
- 1/2 cup mushrooms, diced
- 1/4 cup onion, finely chopped
- 1/4 cup shredded cheese (optional, or use dairyfree cheese)
- 1 tablespoon olive oil
- Salt and pepper to taste
- 1/2 teaspoon garlic powder
- 1/2 teaspoon paprika

TIPS

These egg muffins can be stored in the fridge for up to 4 days or frozen for up to 2 months, making them perfect for meal prep.
Feel free to experiment with other vegetables or addins,

INSTRUCTIONS

- 1. Preheat the oven to 350°F (175°C). Spray a muffin tin with nonstick spray
- 2. In a small skillet, heat olive oil over medium heat. Add onions and mushrooms, sautéing for 3–4 minutes until softened. Stir in the spinach and cook for another minute.
- 3. In a mixing bowl, whisk together eggs, almond milk, garlic powder, paprika, salt, and pepper until fully combined.
- 4. Divide the sautéed vegetables evenly into the muffin tin cups.
- 5. Pour the egg mixture over the vegetables, filling each muffin cup about 3/4 full. Sprinkle shredded cheese on top, if using.
- 6. Bake for 15–20 minutes, or until the egg muffins are set and lightly golden on top.
- 7. Let cool slightly, then remove from the muffin tin and serve warm,

AVOCADO TOAST WITH SMOKED SALMON

PREP TIME
5 minutes

CHILL TIME
0 minutes

SERVING SIZE
2 servings

YIELD
......

NUTRITIONAL VALUE
- Calories: 360 | Protein: 20g
- Carbohydrates: 30g | Fat: 18g
- Fiber: 10g | Sugar: 1g

INGREDIENT

- 2 slices wholegrain bread
- 1 ripe avocado
- 4 ounces smoked salmon
- 1 tablespoon cream cheese (optional)
- 1 tablespoon lemon juice
- Salt and pepper to taste
- 1/4 teaspoon red pepper flakes (optional)
- Fresh dill or chives for garnish (optional)

TIPS

For added flavor, you can incorporate sliced radishes or cucumber on top of the avocado.
If you prefer a spicier kick, consider adding a few drops of hot sauce.
Choose highquality smoked salmon for the best flavor and nutritional benefits.

INSTRUCTIONS

- 1. Toast the wholegrain bread slices until golden brown and crispy.
- 2. While the bread is toasting, cut the avocado in half, remove the pit, and scoop the flesh into a bowl.
- 3. Add lemon juice, salt, and pepper to the avocado, then mash it with a fork until smooth but still slightly chunky.
- 4. Once the toast is ready, spread cream cheese on each slice if using.
- 5. Top each toast with the mashed avocado, spreading it evenly.
- 6. Lay smoked salmon over the avocado mixture, folding it if necessary for a nicer presentation.
- 7. Garnish with red pepper flakes and fresh herbs if desired, and serve immediately.

ALMOND BUTTER AND BANANA TOAST WITH CHIA SEEDS

PREP TIME
5 minutes

COOK TIME
0 minutes

SERVING SIZE
2 servings

YIELD
......

NUTRITIONAL VALUE
- Calories: 350 | Protein: 12g
- Carbohydrates: 45g | Fat: 14g
- Fiber: 8g | Sugar: 6g

INGREDIENT

- 2 slices wholegrain bread
- 4 tablespoons almond butter
- 1 ripe banana, sliced
- 2 tablespoons chia seeds
- 1 tablespoon honey or maple syrup (optional)
- Cinnamon for dusting (optional)

TIPS

Feel free to use other nut butters like peanut butter or cashew butter if preferred. For added crunch, you can top the toast with crushed nuts or seeds of your choice. Using a ripe banana enhances sweetness and creaminess, making it a perfect pairing with almond butter.

INSTRUCTIONS

- 1. Toast the wholegrain bread slices until golden brown and crispy.
- 2. While the bread is toasting, slice the banana into thin rounds.
- 3. Once the toast is ready, spread 2 tablespoons of almond butter on each slice of toast.
- 4. Arrange the banana slices evenly over the almond butter.
- 5. Sprinkle chia seeds on top of the banana slices for added texture and nutrition.
- 6. Drizzle honey or maple syrup over the toast if desired for added sweetness.
- 7. Dust with a sprinkle of cinnamon for a warm flavor, and serve immediately.

Chapter 3

HIGH PROTEIN HIGH FIBER RECIPES

SMOOTHIES AND JUICE

CARROT CAKE SMOOTHIE

PREP TIME
5 minutes

CHILL TIME
0 minutes (blend and serve)

SERVING SIZE
2 servings

YIELD
......

NUTRITIONAL VALUE

- Calories: 180 | Protein: 4g
- Carbohydrates: 36g | Fat: 5g
- Fiber: 8g | Sugar: 12g

INGREDIENT

- 1/2 cup shredded carrots
- 1 frozen banana
- 1 scoop vanilla protein powder
- 1/2 teaspoon cinnamon
- 1/2 teaspoon nutmeg
- 1/2 cup unsweetened almond milk
- 1 tablespoon chia seeds

INSTRUCTIONS

- 1. Add the shredded carrots, banana, protein powder, and almond milk into a blender.
- 2. Sprinkle in the cinnamon and nutmeg.
- 3. Blend on high until smooth.
- 4. Taste and adjust spices if needed.
- 5. Pour into a glass and enjoy your "carrot cake" in a smoothie

TIPS

For a protein boost, consider adding a scoop of protein powder or Greek yogurt. Top with crushed walnuts for a crunchy texture; just add ice for a chill effect.
Feel free to add a handful of spinach for extra nutrients without altering the flavor significantly.

GREEN DETOX SMOOTHIE

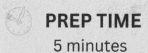
PREP TIME
5 minutes

CHILL TIME
0 minutes (blend and serve)

SERVING SIZE
2 servings

YIELD
......

NUTRITIONAL VALUE
- Calories: 140 | Protein: 3g
- Carbohydrates: 30g | Fat: 2g
- Fiber: 7g | Sugar: 12g

INGREDIENT

- 1 cup kale or spinach (fresh or frozen)
- 1/2 frozen banana
- 1/2 green apple, cored and diced
- 1/2 cucumber, diced
- 1 tablespoon lemon juice
- 1 cup coconut water (or almond milk)
- 1 tablespoon flaxseeds or chia seeds
- 1/2 inch piece of fresh ginger (optional)

TIPS

If you find the smoothie too bitter, consider adding a medjool date for natural sweetness.
Adding a scoop of protein powder or nut butter can increase satiety.
For added detox benefits, incorporate a tablespoon of spirulina powder

INSTRUCTIONS

- 1. In a blender, combine the kale or spinach, frozen banana, green apple, cucumber, lemon juice, coconut water, flaxseeds, and ginger (if using).
- 2. Blend on high until smooth and creamy. Add more coconut water if needed for a thinner consistency.
- 3. Taste and adjust sweetness with a small amount of honey or agave syrup if desired.
- 4. Pour into glasses and serve immediately, optionally garnished with cucumber slices or apple wedges.

TURMERIC GINGER ZINGER

PREP TIME
5 minutes

CHILL TIME
0 minutes (blend and serve)

SERVING SIZE
2 servings

YIELD
......

NUTRITIONAL VALUE
- Calories: 180 | Protein: 2g
- Carbohydrates: 39g | Fat: 5g
- Fiber: 3g | Sugar: 24g

INGREDIENT

- 1/2 cup coconut milk (or almond milk)
- 1/2 cup pineapple chunks (fresh or frozen)
- 1 ripe banana
- 1 teaspoon ground turmeric
- 1/2 inch piece of fresh ginger, peeled and grated (or 1/2 teaspoon ground ginger)
- 1 tablespoon honey or maple syrup (optional)
- 1/2 teaspoon black pepper (to enhance turmeric absorption)

TIPS
If you prefer a colder drink, use frozen pineapple chunks or add ice.
For an extra kick, consider adding cayenne pepper to enhance the zinger effect.

INSTRUCTIONS

- 1. In a blender, combine coconut milk, pineapple chunks, banana, turmeric, grated ginger, honey (if using), and black pepper.
- 2. Blend on high until smooth and creamy. If the mixture is too thick, add more coconut milk until the desired consistency is achieved.
- 3. Taste and adjust sweetness, adding more honey if desired.
- 4. Pour into glasses and serve immediately, garnished with a sprinkle of turmeric or a slice of pineapple.

EQUIPMENT NEEDED:

- Blender
- Measuring cups and spoons
- Glasses for serving
- Fine grater (for ginger)

CHOCOLATE CHERRY ALMOND SMOOTHIE

PREP TIME
5 minutes

CHILL TIME
0 minutes (blend and serve)

SERVING SIZE
2 servings

YIELD
......

NUTRITIONAL VALUE
- Calories: 260 | Protein: 7g
- Carbohydrates: 38g | Fat: 10g
- Fiber: 6g | Sugar: 20g

INGREDIENT

- 1 cup frozen cherries
- 1 ripe banana
- 1 tablespoon unsweetened cocoa powder
- 2 tablespoons almond butter
- 1 cup unsweetened almond milk (or milk of choice)
- 1 tablespoon honey or maple syrup (optional)
- 1/2 teaspoon vanilla extract (optional)

TIPS
For a protein boost, consider adding a scoop of protein powder or Greek yogurt.
You can substitute fresh cherries if preferred; just add ice for a chill effect.
To enhance the chocolate flavor, add a pinch of espresso powder.

INSTRUCTIONS

- 1. In a blender, combine frozen cherries, banana, cocoa powder, almond butter, almond milk, honey (if using), and vanilla extract.
- 2. Blend on high until smooth and creamy. If the smoothie is too thick, add a bit more almond milk to achieve the desired consistency.
- 3. Taste and adjust sweetness if needed by adding more honey or syrup.
- 4. Pour into glasses and serve immediately, optionally garnished with a few whole cherries or a sprinkle of cocoa powder.

EQUIPMENT NEEDED:
- Blender
- Measuring cups and spoons
- Glasses for serving

TROPICAL INFLAMMATION FIGHTER

PREP TIME
5 minutes

CHILL TIME
0 minutes (blend and serve)

SERVING SIZE
2 servings

YIELD
......

NUTRITIONAL VALUE

- Calories: 200 | Protein: 3g
- Carbohydrates: 48g | Fat: 1g
- Fiber: 4g | Sugar: 36g

INGREDIENT

- 1/2 cup fresh or frozen mango chunks
- 1/2 cup fresh or frozen pineapple chunks
- 1 ripe banana
- 1 cup coconut water (or almond milk)
- 1 tablespoon fresh lime juice
- 1 teaspoon fresh turmeric, grated (or 1/2 teaspoon ground turmeric)
- 1/2 inch piece of fresh ginger, peeled and grated (or 1/2 teaspoon ground ginger)
- Optional: 1 tablespoon honey or agave syrup for sweetness

TIPS

For an extra refreshing twist, add a handful of fresh mint leaves before blending.
If you prefer a colder smoothie, use frozen fruit or add ice.

INSTRUCTIONS

- 1. In a blender, combine mango, pineapple, banana, coconut water, lime juice, turmeric, and ginger.
- 2. Blend on high until smooth and creamy. If the smoothie is too thick, add a bit more coconut water until you reach the desired consistency.
- 3. Taste and adjust sweetness by adding honey or agave syrup if desired.
- 4. Pour into glasses and serve immediately, optionally garnished with a slice of lime or pineapple.

EQUIPMENT NEEDED:

- Blender
- Measuring cups and spoons
- Glasses for serving

BEET AND BERRY JUICE BOOSTER

 PREP TIME
10 minutes

 CHILL TIME
0 minutes (juice and serve)

 SERVING SIZE
2 servings

YIELD
......

NUTRITIONAL VALUE

- Calories: 130 | Protein: 2g
- Carbohydrates: 31g | Fat: 0g
- Fiber: 3g | Sugar: 18g

INGREDIENT

- 1 medium beet, peeled and chopped
- 1 cup mixed berries (strawberries, blueberries, raspberries)
- 1 apple, cored and chopped
- 1/2 inch piece of fresh ginger, peeled
- 1 tablespoon fresh lemon juice
- 12 teaspoons honey or agave syrup (optional)
- Water (as needed for blending)

TIPS

To make this juice even more nutrientdense, consider adding a handful of spinach or kale before blending.
If you prefer a colder beverage, chill the ingredients beforehand or serve over ice.
Always wash the beets thoroughly to remove any dirt and pesticides.

INSTRUCTIONS

- 1. If using a juicer, process the chopped beet, mixed berries, apple, and ginger through the juicer.
- 2. If using a blender, combine the chopped beet, mixed berries, apple, ginger, and a splash of water. Blend until smooth.
- 3. If using a blender, strain the mixture through a fine mesh strainer or cheesecloth to remove pulp for a smoother juice.
- 4. Stir in the fresh lemon juice and honey or agave syrup if using.
- 5. Pour into glasses and serve immediately, optionally garnished with a few whole berries or a lemon slice.

EQUIPMENT NEEDED:

- Juicer (or highspeed blender)
- Measuring cups
- Strainer (if using a blender)
- Glasses for serving

GREEN GODDESS JUICE

PREP TIME
10 minutes

CHILL TIME
0 minutes (juice and serve)

SERVING SIZE
2 servings

YIELD
......

NUTRITIONAL VALUE

- Calories: 70 | Protein: 2g
- Carbohydrates: 15g | Fat: 0g
- Fiber: 2g | Sugar: 8g

INGREDIENT

- 1 cucumber, chopped
- 2 green apples, cored and chopped
- 1 cup spinach or kale leaves
- 1/2 lemon, juiced
- 1inch piece of fresh ginger, peeled
- 1 tablespoon fresh parsley (optional)
- Water (as needed for blending)

TIPS

For added sweetness, include a medjool date when blending.
If you want a little kick, add a pinch of cayenne pepper.
Chill the juice ingredients beforehand for a refreshing experience.

INSTRUCTIONS

- 1. If using a juicer, process the cucumber, green apples, spinach or kale, lemon juice, ginger, and parsley through the juicer.
- 2. If using a blender, combine all ingredients with a splash of water and blend until smooth.
- 3. If using a blender, strain the mixture through a fine mesh strainer or cheesecloth to remove pulp for a smoother juice.
- 4. Taste the juice and adjust acidity by adding more lemon juice if desired.
- 5. Pour into glasses and serve immediately, garnished with a slice of cucumber or a sprig of parsley.

EQUIPMENT NEEDED:

- Juicer (or highspeed blender)
- Measuring cups
- Strainer (if using a blender)
- Glasses for serving

WATERMELON MINT REFRESHER

PREP TIME
10 minutes

CHILL TIME
0 minutes (juice and serve)

SERVING SIZE
2 servings

YIELD
......

NUTRITIONAL VALUE

- Calories: 60 | Protein: 1g
- Carbohydrates: 15g | Fat: 0g
- Fiber: 1g | Sugar: 12g

INGREDIENT

- 4 cups watermelon, chopped (seeds removed)
- 1/2 cup fresh mint leaves
- 1 lime, juiced
- Optional: a pinch of sea salt

INSTRUCTIONS

- 1. If using a juicer, process the chopped watermelon, mint leaves, and lime juice through the juicer.
- 2. If using a blender, blend the watermelon, mint leaves, and lime juice until smooth.
- 3. If using a blender, strain the mixture through a fine mesh strainer or cheesecloth to remove pulp for a smoother juice.
- 4. Taste and adjust flavors by adding a pinch of sea salt to enhance sweetness.
- 5. Pour into glasses and serve immediately, optionally garnished with mint sprigs or lime wedges.

TIPS

For a fizzy twist, top the juice with sparkling water before serving.
You can also blend in a little cucumber for extra hydration.
Serve over ice for an extra refreshing treat.

EQUIPMENT NEEDED:

- Juicer (or highspeed blender)
- Measuring cups
- Strainer (if using a blender)
- Glasses for serving

PINEAPPLE TURMERIC ELIXIR

 PREP TIME
10 minutes

 CHILL TIME
0 minutes (juice and serve)

SERVING SIZE
2 servings

YIELD
......

NUTRITIONAL VALUE
- Calories: 120 | Protein: 1g
- Carbohydrates: 30g Fat: 0g
- Fiber: 1g | Sugar: 24g

INGREDIENT

- 2 cups fresh pineapple, chopped
- 1/2 inch piece of fresh turmeric, peeled (or 1 teaspoon ground turmeric)
- 1/2 inch piece of fresh ginger, peeled
- 1 lime, juiced
- 1 tablespoon honey or agave syrup (optional)
- Water (as needed for blending)

INSTRUCTIONS

- 1. If using a juicer, process the pineapple, turmeric, ginger, and lime juice through the juicer.
- 2. If using a blender, combine all ingredients with a splash of water and blend until smooth.
- 3. If using a blender, strain the mixture through a fine mesh strainer or cheesecloth to remove pulp for a smoother juice.
- 4. Taste and adjust sweetness by adding honey or agave syrup if desired.
- 5. Pour into glasses and serve immediately, garnished with a slice of pineapple or lime.

EQUIPMENT NEEDED:
- Juicer (or highspeed blender)
- Measuring cups
- Strainer (if using a blender)
- Glasses for serving

TIPS

For a spicier flavor, increase the amount of ginger or add a pinch of black pepper to enhance turmeric absorption.
You can add coconut water for added electrolytes and a tropical flavor.
Serve chilled for the best refreshing effect.

Chapter 3

HIGH PROTEIN HIGH FIBER

SOUPS AND STEWS

TUSCAN WHITE BEAN AND KALE SOUP

PREP TIME
10 minutes

COOK TIME
30 minutes

SERVING SIZE
4 servings

YIELD
......

NUTRITIONAL VALUE

- Calories: 210 | Protein: 10g
- Carbohydrates: 35g | Fat: 5g
- Fiber: 10g | Sugar: 4g

INGREDIENT

- 1 tablespoon olive oil
- 1 medium onion, diced
- 2 cloves garlic, minced
- 2 carrots, diced
- 2 celery stalks, diced
- 1 teaspoon dried thyme
- 1 teaspoon dried rosemary
- 1 can (15 oz) white beans (cannellini or great northern), drained and rinsed
- 4 cups vegetable broth
- 2 cups kale, chopped (stems removed)
- 1 can (14.5 oz) diced tomatoes, with juice

TIPS

This soup can be made ahead of time and freezes well for future meals.

INSTRUCTIONS

- 1. Heat olive oil in a large pot over medium heat. Add diced onion and sauté for 34 minutes until translucent.
- 2. Stir in garlic, carrots, and celery; cook for an additional 5 minutes, until the vegetables begin to soften.
- 3. Add thyme, rosemary, and white beans, mixing well to combine.
- 4. Pour in the vegetable broth and diced tomatoes (with juices); bring to a boil.
- 5. Reduce heat and let simmer for about 15 minutes, allowing the flavors to meld together.
- 6. Stir in the chopped kale and continue to simmer for another 5 minutes, or until the kale is tender.

ROASTED BUTTERNUT SQUASH AND TURMERIC SOUP

PREP TIME
15 minutes

COOK TIME
40 minutes

SERVING SIZE
2 servings

YIELD
......

NUTRITIONAL VALUE
- Calories: 250 | Protein: 5g
- Carbohydrates: 30g | Fat: 14g
- Fiber: 4g | Sugar: 6g

INGREDIENT

- 1 medium butternut squash, peeled, seeded, and cubed
- 2 tablespoons olive oil
- 1 teaspoon ground turmeric
- 1 teaspoon ground ginger
- Salt and pepper to taste
- 1 onion, diced
- 3 cups vegetable broth
- 1 can (14 oz) coconut milk
- Optional: fresh cilantro for garnish

TIPS

Add a splash of lime juice before serving for a zesty flavor boost.
This soup can be made thicker by reducing the amount of broth added.
For added texture, consider topping with roasted pumpkin seeds.

INSTRUCTIONS

- 1. Preheat the oven to 400°F (200°C). Place cubed butternut squash on a baking sheet and drizzle with 1 tablespoon of olive oil, turmeric, ginger, salt, and pepper. Toss to coat.
- 2. Roast in the oven for about 2530 minutes or until the squash is tender and slightly caramelized.
- 3. In a large pot, heat the remaining olive oil over medium heat. Add diced onion and sauté for 5 minutes until translucent.
- 4. Add the roasted butternut squash to the pot, along with vegetable broth. Bring to a simmer.
- 5. Use an immersion blender to puree the soup until smooth. Alternatively, transfer to a blender in batches and blend until smooth.
- 6. Stir in the coconut milk, and adjust the seasoning as needed.
- 7. Serve hot, garnished with fresh cilantro if desired.

HEALING MISO VEGETABLE SOUP

PREP TIME
10 minutes

COOK TIME
15 minutes

SERVING SIZE
4 servings

YIELD
......

NUTRITIONAL VALUE

- Calories: 130 | Protein: 6g
- Carbohydrates: 20g | Fat: 3g
- Fiber: 4g | Sugar: 3g

INGREDIENT

- 4 cups vegetable broth
- 2 tablespoons miso paste (white or yellow)
- 1 cup mushrooms, sliced
- 1 cup bok choy, chopped
- 1 cup carrots, sliced
- 1 cup broccoli florets
- 1inch piece of ginger, grated
- 2 green onions, sliced (for garnish)
- Optional: tofu, cubed

TIPS

For a heartier soup, add quinoa or rice.
Adjust the amount of miso based on your taste preference—start with less and add more if desired.
This soup is best enjoyed fresh but can be stored in the refrigerator for a couple of days.

INSTRUCTIONS

- 1. In a large pot, bring the vegetable broth to a gentle simmer over medium heat.
- 2. In a small bowl, whisk together the miso paste and a ladleful of warm broth until smooth. Set aside.
- 3. Add mushrooms, bok choy, carrots, broccoli, and grated ginger to the pot. Cook for about 57 minutes until the vegetables are tender.
- 4. If using tofu, add it to the pot during the last few minutes of cooking to warm through.
- 5. Stir in the miso mixture and remove from heat; do not boil after adding miso to preserve its probiotic properties.
- 6. Serve hot, garnished with sliced green onions.

HEARTY LENTIL AND VEGETABLE STEW

PREP TIME
10 minutes

COOK TIME
15 minutes

SERVING SIZE
4 servings

YIELD
......

NUTRITIONAL VALUE

- Calories: 220 | Protein: 12g
- Carbohydrates: 36g | Fat: 3g
- Fiber: 10g | Sugar: 5g

INGREDIENT

- 1 tablespoon olive oil
- 1 onion, diced
- 2 cloves garlic, minced
- 2 carrots, diced
- 2 celery stalks, diced
- 1 red bell pepper, diced
- 1 cup green or brown lentils, rinsed
- 4 cups vegetable broth
- 1 can (14.5 oz) diced tomatoes, with juices
- 2 teaspoons dried thyme
- 1 teaspoon dried oregano
- 2 cups spinach, chopped
- Salt and pepper to taste
- Optional: fresh parsley for garnish

TIPS

Feel free to add other vegetables like zucchini or potatoes for added nutrition.

INSTRUCTIONS

- 1. Heat the olive oil in a large pot over medium heat. Add the diced onion and sauté for 45 minutes until translucent.
- 2. Stir in the garlic, carrots, celery, and red bell pepper; cook for another 5 minutes until the vegetables soften.
- 3. Add the rinsed lentils, vegetable broth, diced tomatoes (with juices), thyme, and oregano. Bring to a boil.
- 4. Reduce heat to low, cover, and simmer for 2530 minutes, or until the lentils are tender.
- 5. Stir in the chopped spinach and cook for an additional 5 minutes until wilted.
- 6. Season with salt and pepper to taste.
- 7. Serve hot, garnished with fresh parsley if desired.

MOROCCAN CHICKPEA AND SWEET POTATO STEW

PREP TIME
10 minutes

COOK TIME
30 minutes

SERVING SIZE
4 servings

YIELD
......

NUTRITIONAL VALUE
- Calories: 220 | Protein: 12g
- Carbohydrates: 36g | Fat: 3g
- Fiber: 10g | Sugar: 5g

INGREDIENT

- 1 tablespoon olive oil
- 1 onion, diced
- 2 cloves garlic, minced
- 1 inch fresh ginger, minced
- 1 large sweet potato, peeled and cubed
- 1 can (15 oz) chickpeas, drained and rinsed
- 1 can (14.5 oz) diced tomatoes, with juices
- 2 cups vegetable broth
- 1 teaspoon ground cumin
- 1 teaspoon ground coriander
- 1 teaspoon ground cinnamon
- 1/2 teaspoon cayenne pepper (optional, for heat)
- 2 cups spinach or kale, chopped
- Salt and pepper to taste
- Optional: fresh cilantro or parsley for garnish

INSTRUCTIONS

- 1. Heat the olive oil in a large pot over medium heat. Add the diced onion and sauté for 45 minutes until translucent.
- 2. Stir in the garlic and ginger, cooking for an additional 12 minutes until fragrant.
- 3. Add the cubed sweet potato, chickpeas, diced tomatoes (with juices), vegetable broth, cumin, coriander, cinnamon, and cayenne pepper (if using).
- 4. Bring the mixture to a boil, then reduce heat to low and cover. Simmer for 20 minutes or until the sweet potatoes are tender.
- 5. Stir in the chopped spinach or kale and cook for another 5 minutes until wilted.
- 6. Season with salt and pepper to taste.
- 7. Serve hot, garnished with fresh cilantro or parsley if desired.

TURKEY AND VEGETABLE SOUP WITH HERBS

PREP TIME
10 minutes

COOK TIME
30 minutes

SERVING SIZE
4 servings

YIELD
......

NUTRITIONAL VALUE

- Calories: 220 | Protein: 12g
- Carbohydrates: 36g | Fat: 3g
- Fiber: 10g | Sugar: 5g

INGREDIENT

- 1 tablespoon olive oil
- 1 pound ground turkey
- 1 onion, diced
- 2 cloves garlic, minced
- 2 carrots, diced
- 2 celery stalks, diced
- 1 zucchini, diced
- 4 cups lowsodium chicken or vegetable broth
- 1 can (14.5 oz) diced tomatoes, with juices
- 1 teaspoon dried thyme
- 1 teaspoon dried oregano
- Salt and pepper to taste
- 2 cups fresh spinach or kale
- Optional: fresh parsley for garnish

TIPS

You can add other vegetables such as bell peppers or green beans for extra nutrition.

INSTRUCTIONS

- 1. Heat olive oil in a large pot over medium heat. Add the ground turkey and cook until browned, breaking it up with a spoon, about 57 minutes.
- 2. Add the diced onion and cook until translucent, about 4 minutes.
- 3. Stir in the garlic, carrots, celery, and zucchini; cook for an additional 5 minutes until the vegetables soften.
- 4. Pour in the broth and diced tomatoes (with juices). Add thyme, oregano, salt, and pepper; bring to a boil.
- 5. Reduce heat to low and let simmer for about 1520 minutes, allowing the flavors to meld together.
- 6. Stir in the spinach or kale and cook for another 5 minutes until wilted.
- 7. Serve hot, garnished with fresh parsley if desired.

SLOW COOKER CHICKEN AND WILD RICE SOUP

PREP TIME
10 minutes

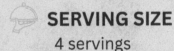

COOK TIME
30 minutes

SERVING SIZE
4 servings

YIELD
......

NUTRITIONAL VALUE
- Calories: 220 | Protein: 12g
- Carbohydrates: 36g | Fat: 3g
- Fiber: 10g | Sugar: 5g

INGREDIENT

- 1 pound boneless, skinless chicken breasts or thighs
- 1 cup wild rice, rinsed
- 1 onion, diced
- 2 cloves garlic, minced
- 3 carrots, diced
- 3 celery stalks, diced
- 4 cups lowsodium chicken broth
- 1 teaspoon dried thyme
- 1 teaspoon dried rosemary
- Salt and pepper to taste
- 1 cup fresh spinach or kale, chopped
- Optional: lemon wedges for serving

TIPS

This soup can be made with leftover roasted chicken for a quicker preparation. Add more broth if you prefer a thinner soup, or let it simmer longer for a thicker consistency.

INSTRUCTIONS

- 1. In the slow cooker, combine the chicken, wild rice, onion, garlic, carrots, and celery.
- 2. Pour in the chicken broth and add thyme, rosemary, salt, and pepper.
- 3. Cover and cook on low for 68 hours or high for 34 hours, until the chicken is cooked through and the rice is tender.
- 4. Remove the chicken, shred it using two forks, and return it to the slow cooker.
- 5. Stir in the fresh spinach or kale and let it wilt for a few minutes before serving.
- 6. Taste and adjust seasoning as needed.
- 7. Serve hot with lemon wedges for an added burst of flavor, if desired.

MEDITERRANEAN FISH STEW

PREP TIME
10 minutes

COOK TIME
30 minutes

SERVING SIZE
4 servings

YIELD

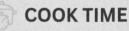
......

NUTRITIONAL VALUE

- Calories: 220 | Protein: 12g
- Carbohydrates: 36g | Fat: 3g
- Fiber: 10g | Sugar: 5g

INGREDIENT

- 2 tablespoons olive oil
- 1 onion, diced
- 2 cloves garlic, minced
- 1 red bell pepper, diced
- 1 zucchini, diced
- 1 can (14.5 oz) diced tomatoes, with juices
- 2 cups lowsodium vegetable broth
- 1 teaspoon dried oregano
- 1 teaspoon smoked paprika
- 1/2 teaspoon red pepper flakes (optional)
- 1 pound white fish fillets (like cod or haddock), cut into chunks
- 1 cup shrimp, peeled and deveined
- 2 cups fresh spinach or kale, chopped
- Salt and pepper to taste
- Optional: fresh parsley and lemon wedges for garnish

INSTRUCTIONS

- 1. Heat olive oil in a large pot over medium heat. Add the diced onion and sauté for 45 minutes until translucent.
- 2. Stir in the garlic and cook for another minute until fragrant.
- 3. Add the red bell pepper and zucchini; cook for 34 minutes until the vegetables soften.
- 4. Pour in the diced tomatoes (with juices), vegetable broth, oregano, smoked paprika, and red pepper flakes (if using). Bring to a boil.
- 5. Reduce heat and simmer for 10 minutes, allowing the flavors to meld.
- 6. Gently add the fish and shrimp to the pot; simmer for an additional 57 minutes until the fish is cooked through and opaque.
- 7. Stir in the chopped spinach or kale and season with salt and pepper to taste.

SALMON AND DILL CHOWDER

PREP TIME
10 minutes

COOK TIME
30 minutes

SERVING SIZE
4 servings

YIELD
......

NUTRITIONAL VALUE

- Calories: 220 | Protein: 12g
- Carbohydrates: 36g | Fat: 3g
- Fiber: 10g | Sugar: 5g

INGREDIENT

- 1 tablespoon olive oil
- 1 onion, diced
- 2 cloves garlic, minced
- 2 cups potatoes, diced
- 4 cups lowsodium vegetable broth
- 1 cup unsweetened almond milk or coconut milk
- 1 pound salmon fillet, skin removed and cut into chunks
- 1 cup corn (fresh, frozen, or canned)
- 2 tablespoons fresh dill, chopped (or 1 tablespoon dried dill)
- Salt and pepper to taste
- Optional: lemon wedges for serving

INSTRUCTIONS

- 1. Heat olive oil in a large pot over medium heat. Add the diced onion and sauté for 45 minutes until translucent.
- 2. Stir in the garlic and cook for another minute until fragrant.
- 3. Add the diced potatoes and vegetable broth; bring to a boil. Reduce heat and simmer for 1520 minutes until the potatoes are tender.
- 4. Stir in the almond milk or coconut milk, salmon chunks, corn, and dill. Cook for an additional 10 minutes until the salmon is cooked through and flakes easily.
- 5. Season with salt and pepper to taste.
- 6. Serve hot with lemon wedges for a fresh burst of flavor.

Chapter 4

HIGH PROTEIN HIGH FIBER

SALADS AND DRESSINGS

ROASTED BEET AND WALNUT SALAD WITH GOAT CHEESE

PREP TIME
15 minutes

COOK TIME
30 minutes

SERVING SIZE
4 servings

YIELD
......

NUTRITIONAL VALUE

- Calories: 280 | Protein: 8g
- Carbohydrates: 22g | Fat: 20g
- Fiber: 5g | Sugar: 6g

INGREDIENT

- 4 medium beets, scrubbed and trimmed
- 1 tablespoon olive oil
- Salt and pepper to taste
- 4 cups mixed salad greens (arugula, spinach, or mesclun)
- 1/2 cup walnuts, toasted
- 4 oz goat cheese, crumbled
- 1/4 cup balsamic vinaigrette (storebought or homemade)

TIPS

For added sweetness, try roasting the beets with a drizzle of honey or maple syrup. This salad can be made ahead of time; just add the dressing right before serving to keep the greens crisp.

INSTRUCTIONS

- 1. Preheat the oven to 400°F (200°C). Line a baking sheet with parchment paper.
- 2. Wrap each beet in aluminum foil and place them on the baking sheet. Roast in the oven for about 3040 minutes until tender. Let cool, then peel and slice.
- 3. In a mixing bowl, combine the salad greens, roasted beets, toasted walnuts, and crumbled goat cheese.
- 4. Drizzle the balsamic vinaigrette over the salad and gently toss to combine. Season with salt and pepper to taste.
- 5. Serve immediately on individual salad plates, garnished with extra walnuts and goat cheese if desired.

THREEBEAN SALAD WITH FRESH BASIL AND OLIVE OIL

PREP TIME
15 minutes

COOK TIME
0 minutes

SERVING SIZE
4 servings

YIELD
......

NUTRITIONAL VALUE

- Calories: 210 | Protein: 10g
- Carbohydrates: 30g | Fat: 7g
- Fiber: 9g | Sugar: 2g

INGREDIENT

- 1 cup canned chickpeas, drained and rinsed
- 1 cup canned black beans, drained and rinsed
- 1 cup canned kidney beans, drained and rinsed
- 1/2 red onion, finely chopped
- 1/2 cup fresh basil leaves, chopped
- 1/4 cup cherry tomatoes, halved
- 1/4 cup olive oil
- 2 tablespoons red wine vinegar
- Salt and pepper to taste

TIPS

Feel free to add diced bell peppers or cucumber for extra crunch and flavor.
It's a great option for meal prep and can be served as a main dish or a side.

INSTRUCTIONS

- 1. In a large mixing bowl, combine the chickpeas, black beans, kidney beans, chopped red onion, chopped basil, and cherry tomatoes.
- 2. In a small bowl, whisk together the olive oil, red wine vinegar, salt, and pepper until well blended.
- 3. Drizzle the dressing over the bean mixture and toss gently to combine, ensuring all ingredients are wellcoated.
- 4. Allow the salad to sit for about 10 minutes to let the flavors meld.
- 5. Serve chilled or at room temperature, garnished with additional basil leaves if desired.

Chapter 5

HIGH PROTEIN HIGH FIBER

MAIN DISHES

STUFFED BELL PEPPERS WITH QUINOA AND BLACK BEANS

PREP TIME
15 minutes

COOK TIME
0 minutes

SERVING SIZE
4 servings

YIELD
......

NUTRITIONAL VALUE
- Calories: 210 | Protein: 10g
- Carbohydrates: 30g | Fat: 7g
- Fiber: 9g | Sugar: 2g

INGREDIENT

- 4 large bell peppers (any color)
- 1 cup quinoa, rinsed
- 2 cups vegetable broth or water
- 1 can (15 oz) black beans, drained and rinsed
- 1 cup corn (fresh, frozen, or canned)
- 1 teaspoon cumin
- 1 teaspoon chili powder
- Salt and pepper to taste
- 1/2 cup diced tomatoes (canned or fresh)
- 1/4 cup cilantro, chopped (for garnish)
- 1/2 cup shredded cheese

TIPS

Feel free to add additional vegetables like zucchini or diced carrots to the filling for more nutrition.

For a spicy kick, add diced jalapeños to the filling.

INSTRUCTIONS

1. Preheat the oven to 375°F (190°C). Slice the tops off the bell peppers and remove the seeds and membranes.

2. In a medium pot, bring the vegetable broth or water to a boil. Add the quinoa, reduce heat, cover, and simmer for about 15 minutes, or until all liquid is absorbed.

3. In a mixing bowl, combine the cooked quinoa, black beans, corn, cumin, chili powder, salt, pepper, and diced tomatoes.

4. Stuff each bell pepper generously with the quinoa and black bean mixture.

5. Pour a small amount of vegetable broth or water into the bottom of the baking dish to keep the peppers moist while baking.

6. Cover the baking dish with foil and bake for 25 minutes. Remove the foil and bake for an additional 5-10 minutes

7. Remove from the oven and let cool slightly

EGGPLANT PARMESAN WITH WHOLE GRAIN BREADCRUMBS

 PREP TIME
15 minutes

 COOK TIME
40 minutes

 SERVING SIZE
4 servings

 YIELD
......

NUTRITIONAL VALUE

- Calories: 290 | Protein: 12g
- Carbohydrates: 34g | Fat: 12g
- Fiber: 7g | Sugar: 6g

INGREDIENT

- 1 large eggplant, sliced into 1/4inch rounds
- 1 cup whole grain breadcrumbs
- 1 cup marinara sauce
- 1/2 cup shredded mozzarella cheese (or vegan cheese)
- 1/4 cup grated Parmesan cheese (or nutritional yeast for vegan option)
- 1/4 cup fresh basil, chopped
- 1 teaspoon Italian seasoning
- Salt and pepper to taste
- Olive oil spray or 2 tablespoons olive oil

TIPS

For added flavor, mix minced garlic into the marinara sauce before layering.
This dish pairs well with a simple side salad or wholegrain pasta.

INSTRUCTIONS

1. Preheat the oven to 400°F (200°C). Line two baking sheets with parchment paper.
2. Arrange the eggplant slices on the baking sheets. Sprinkle with salt and let sit for about 15 minutes to draw out moisture.
3. In a mixing bowl, combine the whole grain breadcrumbs, Italian seasoning, and pepper.
4. Lightly coat each eggplant slice with olive oil spray or brush with olive oil, then dip into the breadcrumb mixture, pressing gently to adhere.
5. Arrange the breaded eggplant slices on the baking sheets and bake for about 25 minutes.
6. In a casserole dish, spread a thin layer of marinara sauce on the bottom. Layer half of the baked eggplant slices, followed by half of the remaining marinara sauce, half of the mozzarella, and half of the Parmesan.
7. Bake for an additional 15 minutes until the cheese is melted and bubbly.

LENTIL AND VEGETABLE CURRY WITH BROWN RICE

PREP TIME
15 minutes

COOK TIME
30 minutes

SERVING SIZE
4 servings

YIELD
......

NUTRITIONAL VALUE

- Calories: 380 |Protein: 15g
- Carbohydrates: 60g | Fat: 7g
- Fiber: 15g | Net Carbs: 45g

INGREDIENT

- For the Curry:
- 1 cup dried lentils (green or brown), rinsed
- 1 tablespoon olive oil
- 1 large onion, chopped
- 3 cloves garlic, minced
- 1 tablespoon fresh ginger, minced
- 1 tablespoon curry powder
- 1 teaspoon ground cumin
- 1 teaspoon turmeric
- 1 can (14 oz) diced tomatoes
- 2 cups vegetable broth
- 1 medium sweet potato, peeled and diced
- 1 zucchini, diced
- 1 cup spinach or kale
- Salt and pepper to taste

FOR THE BROWN RICE:

- 1 cup brown rice
- 2 cups water
- Pinch of salt

INSTRUCTIONS

1. Cook the rice: In a medium pot, combine the brown rice, water, and a pinch of salt. Bring to a boil, reduce the heat to low, cover, and simmer for 25-30 minutes until the rice is cooked through and the water is absorbed.

2. Sauté the aromatics: While the rice cooks, heat the olive oil in a large pot or Dutch oven over medium heat. Add the chopped onion and cook for 4-5 minutes until softened. Stir in the minced garlic and ginger, cooking for another minute until fragrant.

3. Add the spices then Add lentils and vegetables: Pour in the diced tomatoes, vegetable broth, and lentils. Add the sweet potatoes and bring the mixture to a boil. Reduce the heat to a simmer, cover, and cook.

4. Add zucchini and greens: Stir in the zucchini and simmer for another 5 minutes. Finally, stir in the spinach or kale until wilted. Season with salt and pepper to taste.

ROASTED PORTOBELLO MUSHROOM STEAKS WITH HERB SAUCE

PREP TIME
15 minutes

COOK TIME
20 minutes

SERVING SIZE
4 servings

YIELD
......

NUTRITIONAL VALUE
- Calories: 120 | Protein: 4g
- Carbohydrates: 8g | Fat: 9g
- Fiber: 2g | Net Carbs: 6g

INGREDIENT

For the Portobello Steaks:
- 4 large Portobello mushrooms, stems removed
- 2 tablespoons olive oil
- 2 tablespoons balsamic vinegar
- 1 tablespoon soy sauce or tamari (for gluten-free)
- 1 teaspoon smoked paprika
- Salt and pepper to taste

For the Herb Sauce:
- ¼ cup fresh parsley, finely chopped
- ¼ cup fresh cilantro, finely chopped
- 1 clove garlic, minced
- 2 tablespoons olive oil
- 1 tablespoon lemon juice
- Salt and pepper to taste

TIPS
Marination: Let the mushrooms sit in the marinade for 10 minutes before roasting for extra flavor.

INSTRUCTIONS

1. Preheat the oven: Preheat your oven to 400°F (200°C) and line a baking sheet with parchment paper.

2. Marinate the mushrooms: In a small bowl, whisk together the olive oil, balsamic vinegar, soy sauce, smoked paprika, salt, and pepper. Brush this mixture evenly over both sides of the Portobello mushrooms.

3. Roast the mushrooms: Place the mushrooms gill side up on the prepared baking sheet. Roast in the oven for 15–20 minutes, flipping halfway through, until tender and caramelized.

4. Make the herb sauce: While the mushrooms are roasting, prepare the herb sauce. In a small bowl, mix together the parsley, cilantro, garlic, olive oil, lemon juice, salt, and pepper.

5. Serve: Once the mushrooms are done, plate them and drizzle with the fresh herb sauce. Serve immediately, with additional sauce on the side.

TURMERIC AND LEMON ROASTED CHICKEN WITH ROOT VEGETABLES

PREP TIME
15 minutes

COOK TIME
1 hour

SERVING SIZE
4 servings

YIELD
......

NUTRITIONAL VALUE
- Calories: 450 | Protein: 35g
- Carbohydrates: 25g | Fat: 25g
- Fiber: 6g | Net Carbs: 19g

INGREDIENT

For the Chicken:
- 1 whole chicken (about 4 pounds)
- 2 tablespoons olive oil
- 1 tablespoon ground turmeric
- 1 lemon, zested and quartered
- 4 garlic cloves, minced
- 1 teaspoon ground cumin
- 1 teaspoon paprika
- Salt and pepper to taste

For the Vegetables:
- 2 large carrots, peeled and chopped
- 2 parsnips, peeled and chopped
- 1 sweet potato, peeled and cubed
- 1 red onion, quartered
- 2 tablespoons olive oil
- Salt and pepper to taste

TIPS
Crispy skin: To get the skin extra crispy, broil the chicken for the last 5 minutes of roasting.

INSTRUCTIONS

1. Preheat the oven: Preheat your oven to 400°F (200°C).
2. Prepare the chicken: In a small mixing bowl, combine olive oil, turmeric, lemon zest, garlic, cumin, paprika, salt, and pepper. Rub this mixture all over the chicken, ensuring it covers the skin evenly. Stuff the cavity of the chicken with lemon quarters.
3. Prepare the vegetables: In a large bowl, toss the chopped carrots, parsnips, sweet potato, and red onion with olive oil, salt, and pepper.
4. Roast the chicken and vegetables: Place the chicken on top of the vegetables in the roasting pan. Roast in the preheated oven for about 1 hour. Baste the chicken with its juices halfway through cooking if desired.
5. Rest and serve: Once done, remove the chicken from the oven and let it rest for 10 minutes before carving.

TURKEY AND VEGETABLE STIR-FRY WITH GINGER SAUCE

PREP TIME
15 minutes

COOK TIME
15 minutes

SERVING SIZE
4 servings

YIELD
......

NUTRITIONAL VALUE
- Calories: 320 | Protein: 25g
- Carbohydrates: 12g | Fat: 18g
- Fiber: 4g | Net Carbs: 8g

INGREDIENT

For the Stir-Fry:
- 1 pound ground turkey
- 1 tablespoon olive oil or sesame oil
- 1 red bell pepper, sliced
- 1 zucchini, sliced
- 1 carrot, thinly sliced
- 2 cups broccoli florets
- 3 green onions, chopped
- 2 cloves garlic, minced
- Salt and pepper to taste

For the Ginger Sauce:
- ¼ cup soy sauce or tamari (for gluten-free)
- 1 tablespoon fresh ginger, minced
- 1 tablespoon rice vinegar
- 1 tablespoon sesame oil
- 1 tablespoon water
- 1 teaspoon cornstarch or arrowroot powder (for thickening)

INSTRUCTIONS

1. Prepare the sauce: In a small bowl, whisk together the soy sauce, ginger, rice vinegar, sesame oil, honey (if using), water, and cornstarch. Set aside.

2. Cook the turkey: Heat 1 tablespoon of olive oil or sesame oil in a large skillet Add the ground turkey and cook until browned and fully cooked through, about 5-7 minutes. Transfer the cooked turkey to a plate and set aside.

3. Sauté the vegetables: In the same skillet, add the red bell pepper, zucchini, carrot, broccoli, and green onions. Sauté for 5-6 minutes until the vegetables are tender but still crisp. Add the minced garlic and cook for an additional 30 seconds until fragrant.

4. Combine and stir-fry: Return the cooked turkey to the skillet with the vegetables. Pour the ginger sauce over the mixture and stir to coat everything evenly. Cook for another 2-3 minutes

5. Serve

BAKED SALMON WITH DILL AND LEMON

 PREP TIME
15 minutes

 COOK TIME
15-20 minutes

SERVING SIZE
4 servings

 YIELD
......

NUTRITIONAL VALUE

- Calories: 350 | Protein: 35g
- Carbohydrates: 2g | Fat: 23g
- Fiber: 0g | Net Carbs: 2g

INGREDIENT

- 4 salmon fillets (about 6 oz each)
- 2 tablespoons olive oil
- 2 tablespoons fresh lemon juice
- 1 tablespoon fresh dill, chopped (or 1 teaspoon dried dill)
- 1 garlic clove, minced
- 1 lemon, thinly sliced
- Salt and pepper to taste
- Fresh dill sprigs for garnish (optional)

TIPS

Crispier texture: For a slightly crispy top, broil the salmon for the last 2-3 minutes of cooking.

Flavor boost: Marinate the salmon in the dill and lemon mixture for 30 minutes before baking for an extra punch of flavor.

INSTRUCTIONS

1. Preheat the oven: Preheat your oven to 375°F (190°C). Line a baking sheet or dish with parchment paper or aluminum foil.
2. Prepare the salmon: Place the salmon fillets on the prepared baking sheet. Season each fillet with salt and pepper.
3. Make the dill and lemon mixture: In a small bowl, whisk together olive oil, lemon juice, minced garlic, and chopped dill.
4. Coat the salmon: Pour the dill and lemon mixture over the salmon fillets, ensuring each piece is well-coated. Lay thin lemon slices on top of each fillet.
5. Bake the salmon: Bake the salmon in the preheated oven for 15-20 minutes, or until the fish flakes easily with a fork and reaches an internal temperature of 145°F (63°C).
6. Garnish and serve: Once baked, remove the salmon from the oven and garnish with fresh dill sprigs if desired.

MEDITERRANEAN-STYLE GRILLED SHRIMP SKEWERS

PREP TIME
10 minutes (plus 15 minutes marinating time)

COOK TIME
5-7 minutes

SERVING SIZE
4 servings

YIELD
......

NUTRITIONAL VALUE
- Calories: 210 | Protein: 25g
- Carbohydrates: 3g | Fat: 11g
- Fiber: 1g | Net Carbs: 2g

INGREDIENT

- 1 pound large shrimp, peeled and deveined
- 3 tablespoons olive oil
- 2 tablespoons fresh lemon juice
- 1 tablespoon fresh oregano, chopped (or 1 teaspoon dried oregano)
- 2 garlic cloves, minced
- 1 teaspoon paprika
- Salt and pepper to taste
- Lemon wedges for serving
- Fresh parsley for garnish (optional)

TIPS

Perfectly cooked shrimp: Be careful not to overcook the shrimp, as they can become tough. Remove them from the grill as soon as they turn pink and opaque.

Meal pairing: These shrimp skewers pair wonderfully with hummus, tzatziki, or a side of quinoa for a full Mediterranean meal.

INSTRUCTIONS

1. Preheat the grill: Preheat your grill or grill pan to medium-high heat. If using wooden skewers, soak them in water for 15 minutes to prevent burning.

2. Marinate the shrimp: In a small bowl, whisk together olive oil, lemon juice, oregano, garlic, paprika, salt, and pepper. Add the shrimp to the bowl and toss to coat. Allow the shrimp to marinate for 15 minutes.

3. Assemble the skewers: Thread the marinated shrimp onto the skewers, leaving a small amount of space between each shrimp.

4. Grill the shrimp: Grill the shrimp skewers for 2-3 minutes per side, or until the shrimp turn pink and are cooked through.

5. Serve: Remove the shrimp from the grill and transfer to a serving plate. Garnish with fresh parsley and lemon wedges, and serve with a Mediterranean salad or roasted vegetables.

SLOW COOKER GRASS-FED BEEF STEW WITH VEGETABLES

PREP TIME
10 minutes (plus 15 minutes marinating time)

COOK TIME
5-7 minutes

SERVING SIZE
4 servings

YIELD
......

NUTRITIONAL VALUE
- Calories: 360 | Protein: 35g
- Carbohydrates: 20g | Fat: 15g
- Fiber: 4g | Net Carbs: 16g

INGREDIENT

- 2 pounds grass-fed beef stew meat, cubed
- 4 carrots, peeled and chopped
- 3 celery stalks, chopped
- 3 potatoes, chopped (optional for lower-carb, replace with cauliflower)
- 1 onion, diced
- 3 garlic cloves, minced
- 4 cups beef broth (low-sodium)
- 1 tablespoon tomato paste
- 1 teaspoon dried thyme
- 1 teaspoon dried rosemary
- 1 bay leaf
- Salt and pepper to taste

TIPS
Thickening the stew: For a thicker consistency, remove ½ cup of broth, mix with 1 tablespoon of cornstarch, and stir back into the stew for the last 30 minutes of cooking.

INSTRUCTIONS

1. Optional: Sear the beef: For extra flavor, heat olive oil in a large skillet over medium-high heat and sear the beef cubes on all sides. Transfer to the slow cooker.

2. Prepare vegetables: Add the chopped carrots, celery, potatoes (or cauliflower for low-carb), onion, and garlic to the slow cooker.

3. Add seasonings: Stir in the tomato paste, thyme, rosemary, and bay leaf. Season with salt and pepper.

4. Pour in broth: Add the beef broth to the slow cooker, ensuring the ingredients are submerged.

5. Cook low and slow: Cover and cook on low for 6-8 hours, or on high for 4-5 hours, until the beef is tender and the vegetables are cooked through.

6. Finish and serve: Once done, remove the bay leaf, stir the stew, and garnish with fresh parsley before serving.

HERB-CRUSTED LAMB CHOPS WITH ROASTED GARLIC

PREP TIME

10 minutes (plus 15 minutes marinating time)

COOK TIME

15-20 minutes

SERVING SIZE

4 servings

YIELD

......

NUTRITIONAL VALUE

- Calories: 420 | Protein: 30g
- Carbohydrates: 8g | Fat: 30g
- Fiber: 2g | Net Carbs: 6g

INGREDIENT

- 8 lamb chops (about 1 inch thick)
- 2 tablespoons fresh rosemary, chopped (or 1 tablespoon dried rosemary)
- 2 tablespoons fresh thyme, chopped
- 4 garlic cloves, minced
- 3 tablespoons olive oil
- Salt and pepper to taste
- 1 head of garlic, top sliced off
- 1 tablespoon balsamic vinegar (optional)

TIPS

Use a meat thermometer: This ensures your lamb is cooked perfectly—145°F for medium-rare, or cook longer for medium-well.

Flavor boost: Drizzle balsamic vinegar over the roasted garlic for a sweet and tangy addition.

INSTRUCTIONS

1. Preheat the oven: Preheat your oven to 400°F (200°C). Line a baking sheet with aluminum foil.
2. Prepare the lamb chops: In a small bowl, combine chopped rosemary, thyme, garlic, and olive oil. Rub this mixture generously over both sides of the lamb chops.
3. Roast the garlic: Place the garlic head (with the top sliced off) on the baking sheet, drizzle with olive oil, and wrap it in aluminum foil.
4. Cook the lamb: Place the herb-coated lamb chops on the same baking sheet. Roast the lamb chops in the oven for 15-20 minutes.
5. Optional: Sear for a crispy finish: For extra crispiness, sear the lamb chops in a hot skillet for 1-2 minutes on each side after roasting.
6. Serve: Once done, remove the lamb from the oven and let it rest for 5 minutes. Serve the lamb chops with the roasted garlic, squeezing the soft garlic out of the cloves as a spread.

Chapter 6

HIGH PROTEIN HIGH FIBER RECIPES

SIDE DISHES

ROASTED RAINBOW CARROTS WITH TURMERIC AND HONEY

PREP TIME
10 minutes

COOK TIME
25-30 minutes

SERVING SIZE
4 servings

YIELD
......

NUTRITIONAL VALUE
- Calories: 140 | Protein: 1g
- Carbohydrates: 18g | Fat: 7g
- Fiber: 4g | Net Carbs: 14g

INGREDIENT

- 1 pound rainbow carrots, peeled and cut in half lengthwise
- 2 tablespoons olive oil
- 1 tablespoon honey
- 1 teaspoon ground turmeric
- ½ teaspoon ground cumin
- Salt and pepper to taste
- Fresh parsley for garnish (optional)

INSTRUCTIONS

1. Preheat the oven: Preheat your oven to 400°F (200°C) and line a baking sheet with parchment paper.
2. Prepare the carrots: In a mixing bowl, toss the carrots with olive oil, honey, turmeric, cumin, salt, and pepper until well coated.
3. Roast the carrots: Spread the carrots in a single layer on the prepared baking sheet. Roast in the preheated oven for 25-30 minutes, flipping halfway through, until the carrots are tender and slightly caramelized.
4. Garnish and serve: Once done, remove the carrots from the oven and garnish with fresh parsley before serving.

TIPS

Even roasting: Ensure the carrots are in a single layer on the baking sheet to ensure even roasting.
Spice variation: Add a pinch of cinnamon for a sweeter, spiced flavor profile.

GARLIC SAUTÉED GREEN BEANS WITH ALMONDS

PREP TIME
10 minutes

COOK TIME
10 minutes

SERVING SIZE
4 servings

YIELD
......

NUTRITIONAL VALUE

- Calories: 160 | Protein: 4g
- Carbohydrates: 10g | Fat: 12g
- Fiber: 4g | Net Carbs: 6g

INGREDIENT

- 1 pound fresh green beans, trimmed
- 2 tablespoons olive oil
- 3 garlic cloves, minced
- ¼ cup sliced almonds
- Salt and pepper to taste
- Lemon wedges for serving (optional)

EQUIPMENT NEEDED:

- Large skillet
- Wooden spoon or spatula

TIPS

Blanch the beans: To keep the green beans vibrant and crisp, blanch them in boiling water for 2 minutes before sautéing.
Almond alternatives: Swap almonds for slivered hazelnuts or pecans for a different texture and flavor.

INSTRUCTIONS

1. Sauté the garlic: Heat the olive oil in a large skillet over medium heat. Add the minced garlic and cook for 1 minute until fragrant, being careful not to burn.

2. Cook the green beans: Add the green beans to the skillet and sauté for 6-8 minutes, stirring occasionally, until the beans are tender but still slightly crisp.

3. Add almonds: Stir in the sliced almonds during the last 2 minutes of cooking, allowing them to lightly toast.

4. Serve: Remove from heat and season with salt and pepper. Serve with a squeeze of lemon juice if desired.

BAKED SWEET POTATO WEDGES WITH ROSEMARY

PREP TIME
10 minutes

COOK TIME
25-30 minutes

SERVING SIZE
4 servings

YIELD
....

NUTRITIONAL VALUE
- Calories: 180 | Protein: 2g
- Carbohydrates: 28g | Fat: 7g
- Fiber: 5g | Net Carbs: 23g

INGREDIENT

- 2 large sweet potatoes, cut into wedges
- 2 tablespoons olive oil
- 1 teaspoon fresh rosemary, chopped (or ½ teaspoon dried rosemary)
- ½ teaspoon paprika
- Salt and pepper to taste

EQUIPMENT NEEDED:

- Baking sheet
- Parchment paper
- Mixing bowl

TIPS

Crispier wedges: For extra crispiness, increase the oven temperature to 425°F (220°C) for the last 5 minutes of baking.

Dipping sauce: Serve with a side of garlic aioli or Greek yogurt dip for added flavor

INSTRUCTIONS

1. Preheat the oven: Preheat your oven to 400°F (200°C) and line a baking sheet with parchment paper.
2. Season the sweet potatoes: In a large mixing bowl, toss the sweet potato wedges with olive oil, rosemary, paprika, salt, and pepper.
3. Bake the wedges: Spread the sweet potato wedges in a single layer on the prepared baking sheet. Bake for 25-30 minutes, flipping halfway through, until the wedges are crispy on the outside and tender on the inside.
4. Serve: Once baked, remove from the oven and serve immediately.

GRILLED ASPARAGUS WITH LEMON ZEST

PREP TIME
10 minutes

COOK TIME
6-8 minutes

SERVING SIZE
4 servings

YIELD
......

NUTRITIONAL VALUE
- Calories: 100 | Protein: 3g
- Carbohydrates: 6g | Fat: 8g
- Fiber: 3g | Net Carbs: 3g

INGREDIENT

- 1 pound fresh asparagus, trimmed
- 2 tablespoons olive oil
- Zest of 1 lemon
- Salt and pepper to taste
- Lemon wedges for serving

EQUIPMENT NEEDED:

- Grill or grill pan
- Zester or fine grater

TIPS

Char for flavor: Grill the asparagus until you see a bit of char for a smoky flavor.
Alternative seasoning: Try adding a sprinkle of Parmesan cheese for an extra layer of flavor.

INSTRUCTIONS

1. Preheat the grill: Preheat your grill or grill pan to medium-high heat.
2. Season the asparagus: Toss the asparagus with olive oil, salt, and pepper.
3. Grill the asparagus: Grill the asparagus for 3-4 minutes per side, turning occasionally, until slightly charred and tender.
4. Add lemon zest: Remove the asparagus from the grill and sprinkle with lemon zest. Serve immediately with lemon wedges on the side.

QUINOA PILAF WITH HERBS AND LEMON

PREP TIME
10 minutes

COOK TIME
20 minutes

SERVING SIZE
4 servings

YIELD
......

NUTRITIONAL VALUE
- Calories: 180 | Protein: 6g
- Carbohydrates: 30g | Fat: 5g
- Fiber: 3g | Net Carbs: 27g

INGREDIENT

- 1 cup quinoa, rinsed
- 2 cups vegetable broth or water
- 1 tablespoon olive oil
- 1 garlic clove, minced
- 2 tablespoons fresh parsley, chopped
- 1 tablespoon fresh dill, chopped
- Zest of 1 lemon
- 1 tablespoon lemon juice
- Salt and pepper to taste

EQUIPMENT NEEDED:

- Medium saucepan
- Strainer
- Fork for fluffing

TIPS

Additional herbs: Try adding other fresh herbs like cilantro or basil for a different flavor profile.

INSTRUCTIONS

1. Rinse the quinoa: Place the quinoa in a fine mesh strainer and rinse under cold water to remove the bitter coating (saponins).
2. Cook the quinoa: In a medium saucepan, bring the vegetable broth to a boil. Add the quinoa, reduce heat to low, and cover. Simmer for 15 minutes, or until all the liquid is absorbed.
3. Fluff the quinoa: Remove the quinoa from heat and let it sit covered for 5 minutes.
4. Sauté garlic: While the quinoa is cooking, heat the olive oil in a small pan over medium heat. Add the minced garlic and sauté for 1 minute until fragrant, but not browned.
5. Combine and season: Mix the sautéed garlic, fresh parsley, dill, lemon zest, and lemon juice into the fluffed quinoa. Season with salt and pepper to taste.
6. Serve: Serve warm or at room temperature as a side dish.

WILD RICE AND MUSHROOM MEDLEY

PREP TIME
10 minutes

COOK TIME
20 minutes

SERVING SIZE
4 servings

YIELD
......

NUTRITIONAL VALUE
- Calories: 200 | Protein: 7g
- Carbohydrates: 34g | Fat: 6g
- Fiber: 3g | Net Carbs: 31g

INGREDIENT

- 1 cup wild rice, rinsed
- 2 ½ cups vegetable broth or water
- 1 tablespoon olive oil
- 1 small onion, finely chopped
- 2 garlic cloves, minced
- 1 cup cremini mushrooms, sliced
- 1 teaspoon fresh thyme leaves (or ½ teaspoon dried thyme)
- 1 tablespoon fresh parsley, chopped
- Salt and pepper to taste

EQUIPMENT NEEDED:

- Medium saucepan
- Strainer
- Fork for fluffing

TIPS

Add veggies: For a more colorful dish, add sautéed spinach, kale, or roasted bell peppers to the rice and mushroom mixture.

INSTRUCTIONS

1. Cook the wild rice: In a medium saucepan, bring the vegetable broth (or water) to a boil. Add the rinsed wild rice, cover, and reduce heat to low. Simmer for 40-45 minutes, or until the rice is tender and most of the liquid is absorbed.
2. Sauté the vegetables: While the rice is cooking, heat the olive oil in a large skillet over medium heat. Add the chopped onion and garlic, and sauté for 3-4 minutes until softened.
3. Cook the mushrooms: Add the sliced mushrooms to the skillet and cook for another 5-7 minutes, stirring occasionally, until the mushrooms are tender and lightly browned.
4. Combine and season: Once the wild rice is cooked, add it to the skillet with the mushroom mixture. Stir in the fresh thyme and parsley, and season with salt and pepper to taste.
5. Serve: Serve warm as a hearty and flavorful side dish.

SPICED LENTILS WITH CARAMELIZED ONIONS

PREP TIME
10 minutes

COOK TIME
35-40 minutes

SERVING SIZE
4 servings

YIELD
......

NUTRITIONAL VALUE
- Calories: 180 | Protein: 10g
- Carbohydrates: 30g | Fat: 4g
- Fiber: 12g | Net Carbs: 18g

INGREDIENT

- 1 cup green or brown lentils, rinsed
- 2 ½ cups vegetable broth or water
- 1 tablespoon olive oil
- 1 large onion, thinly sliced
- 1 garlic clove, minced
- 1 teaspoon cumin
- 1 teaspoon ground coriander
- ½ teaspoon turmeric
- ¼ teaspoon cinnamon
- 1 tablespoon fresh cilantro, chopped
- Salt and pepper to taste

EQUIPMENT NEEDED:

- Medium saucepan
- Large skillet
- Wooden spoon

TIPS

Texture variation: For a crunch, add toasted nuts like almonds or walnuts on top before serving.

INSTRUCTIONS

1. Cook the lentils: In a medium saucepan, bring the vegetable broth (or water) to a boil. Add the rinsed lentils, reduce heat to low, and simmer for 25-30 minutes until tender but not mushy. Drain excess liquid if necessary.

2. Caramelize the onions: While the lentils cook, heat olive oil in a large skillet over medium heat. Add the sliced onions and cook, stirring occasionally.

3. Add garlic and spices: Add the minced garlic, cumin, coriander, turmeric, and cinnamon to the caramelized onions. Cook for another 2-3 minutes, stirring until fragrant.

4. Combine lentils and onions: Add the cooked lentils to the skillet with the onion mixture.

5. Season and garnish: Season with salt and pepper to taste

6. Serve: Serve warm as a side or as a main dish over rice or with flatbread.

LEMONY GARLIC HUMMUS

PREP TIME
10 minutes

COOK TIME
None

SERVING SIZE
4 servings

YIELD
......

NUTRITIONAL VALUE
- Calories: 150 | Protein: 5g
- Carbohydrates: 13g | Fat: 9g
- Fiber: 4g | Net Carbs: 9g

INGREDIENT

- 1 can (15 oz) chickpeas, drained and rinsed
- 2 tablespoons tahini
- 2 tablespoons olive oil
- 2 garlic cloves, minced
- Juice of 1 lemon
- ¼ teaspoon ground cumin
- ¼ cup water (more if needed for consistency)
- Salt and pepper to taste
- Paprika and olive oil for garnish (optional)

EQUIPMENT NEEDED:

- Food processor or blender
- Small mixing bowl

TIPS

Creamier hummus: For extra smooth hummus, peel the skins off the chickpeas before blending.

INSTRUCTIONS

1. Prepare the chickpeas: Drain and rinse the chickpeas thoroughly. Set aside.
2. Blend the ingredients: In a food processor or blender, combine the chickpeas, tahini, olive oil, minced garlic, lemon juice, cumin, and ¼ cup of water. Blend until smooth. If the hummus is too thick, add more water, one tablespoon at a time, until you reach your desired consistency.
3. Season: Taste the hummus and season with salt and pepper to your preference. Blend again to mix.
4. Serve: Transfer the hummus to a small bowl, drizzle with olive oil, and sprinkle with paprika (if using).
5. Optional: Garnish with fresh herbs like parsley or cilantro for a burst of color and flavor.
6. Enjoy: Serve with fresh vegetables, whole-grain pita, or as a spread on sandwiches.

ROASTED BRUSSELS SPROUTS WITH BUTTERNUT SQUASH AND CRANBERRIES

PREP TIME
10 minutes

COOK TIME
35-40 minutes

SERVING SIZE
4 servings

YIELD
....

NUTRITIONAL VALUE
- Calories: 180 | Protein: 3g
- Carbohydrates: 26g | Fat: 7g
- Fiber: 6g | Net Carbs: 20g

INGREDIENT

- 2 cups Brussels sprouts, trimmed and halved
- 2 cups butternut squash, peeled and cubed
- 2 tablespoons olive oil
- 1 teaspoon ground cinnamon
- ¼ teaspoon nutmeg
- Salt and pepper to taste
- ½ cup dried cranberries (unsweetened if possible)
- 1 tablespoon maple syrup (optional)
- ¼ cup chopped walnuts or pecans (optional for crunch)

TIPS

Make ahead: You can roast the Brussels sprouts and squash in advance, then reheat and add cranberries just before serving.
Flavor boost: Add a sprinkle of balsamic vinegar or balsamic glaze for extra tang.

INSTRUCTIONS

1. Preheat the oven: Preheat your oven to 400°F (200°C).
2. Prepare vegetables: In a large mixing bowl, toss the halved Brussels sprouts and cubed butternut squash with olive oil, cinnamon, nutmeg, salt, and pepper until evenly coated.
3. Roast the vegetables: Spread the vegetables in an even layer on a baking sheet. Roast in the oven for 30-35 minutes, tossing halfway through, until the Brussels sprouts are golden and the squash is tender.
4. Add cranberries: In the last 5 minutes of roasting, sprinkle the dried cranberries over the vegetables to allow them to soften slightly in the heat
5. Serve: Serve warm as a hearty side dish for any meal.

MEDITERRANEAN CHICKPEA AND VEGETABLE MEDLEY

PREP TIME
10 minutes

COOK TIME
20 minutes

SERVING SIZE
4 servings

YIELD
......

NUTRITIONAL VALUE

- Calories: 220 | Protein: 8g
- Carbohydrates: 30g | Fat: 8g
- Fiber: 8g | Net Carbs: 22g

INGREDIENT

- 1 can (15 oz) chickpeas, drained and rinsed
- 1 zucchini, diced
- 1 red bell pepper, diced
- 1 small red onion, finely chopped
- 1 tablespoon olive oil
- 1 garlic clove, minced
- 1 teaspoon dried oregano
- 1 teaspoon ground cumin
- ½ teaspoon smoked paprika
- Juice of 1 lemon
- 2 tablespoons fresh parsley, chopped
- Salt and pepper to taste
- Feta cheese (optional, for garnish)

TIPS

Meal prep: This dish stores well, so you can make it ahead and enjoy as a quick side or main throughout the week.

INSTRUCTIONS

1. Sauté the vegetables: Heat the olive oil in a large skillet over medium heat. Add the chopped red onion, diced zucchini, and bell pepper. Cook for about 5 minutes, stirring occasionally, until the vegetables begin to soften.

2. Add garlic and spices: Stir in the minced garlic, oregano, cumin, and smoked paprika. Cook for another 1-2 minutes until fragrant.

3. Add chickpeas: Add the drained and rinsed chickpeas to the skillet. Stir to combine and cook for another 5-7 minutes, until the chickpeas are heated through and slightly crisp.

4. Season: Squeeze the juice of 1 lemon over the chickpea and vegetable medley. Season with salt and pepper to taste.

5. Garnish and serve: Remove from heat, sprinkle with fresh parsley, and top with crumbled feta cheese (if using). Serve warm as a Mediterranean-inspired side.

Chapter 7

HIGH PROTEIN HIGH FIBER RECIPES

SNACKS AND APPETIZERS

BERRY AND CHIA SEED PUDDING CUPS

 PREP TIME
10 minutes

 CHILL TIME
4 hours or overnight

 SERVING SIZE
4 servings

 YIELD
......

NUTRITIONAL VALUE

- Calories: 150 | Protein: 4g
- Carbohydrates: 17g | Fat: 7g
- Fiber: 7g | Net Carbs: 10g

INGREDIENT

- 1 ½ cups almond milk (or any plant-based milk)
- ¼ cup chia seeds
- 1 tablespoon maple syrup or honey (optional)
- 1 teaspoon vanilla extract
- 1 cup mixed fresh berries (strawberries, blueberries, raspberries)
- 1 tablespoon unsweetened shredded coconut (optional, for topping)
- 1 tablespoon chopped nuts (optional, for topping)

TIPS

Sweetness: Adjust the sweetness to your liking by adding more or less maple syrup or honey.
Variety: Use different fruits, such as mango, kiwi, or pomegranate, for variety.

INSTRUCTIONS

1. Mix the chia pudding: In a medium mixing bowl, whisk together the almond milk, chia seeds, maple syrup (if using), and vanilla extract. Stir well to ensure the chia seeds are evenly distributed.

2. Let it thicken: Cover the bowl and refrigerate for at least 4 hours or overnight. The chia seeds will absorb the liquid and create a pudding-like consistency.

3. Prepare the berries: Just before serving, wash and prepare the fresh berries by slicing any larger fruits like strawberries.

4. Assemble the pudding cups: Once the chia pudding has set, divide it evenly between 4 serving cups or jars. Top each with a generous amount of mixed berries.

5. Optional toppings: Sprinkle each cup with shredded coconut and chopped nuts for added texture and flavor

APPLE SLICES WITH ALMOND BUTTER AND CINNAMON

PREP TIME
5 minutes

CHILL TIME
....

SERVING SIZE
4 servings

YIELD
....

NUTRITIONAL VALUE

- Calories: 250 | Protein: 6g
- Carbohydrates: 30g | Fat: 14g
- Fiber: 8g | Net Carbs: 22g

INGREDIENT

- 1 medium apple (any variety, like Honeycrisp or Granny Smith)
- 2 tablespoons almond butter (unsweetened)
- ½ teaspoon ground cinnamon
- 1 tablespoon chia seeds or hemp seeds (optional, for topping)

EQUIPMENT NEEDED:

- Food processor or blender
- Small mixing bowl

TIPS

Alternative nut butters: Swap almond butter with peanut butter, cashew butter, or sunflower seed butter based on your preference.
Keep apples fresh: If preparing ahead of time, drizzle a little lemon juice on the apple slices to prevent browning.

INSTRUCTIONS

1. Slice the apple: Wash the apple thoroughly and slice it into thin wedges or rounds.
2. Prepare the almond butter: If desired, warm the almond butter slightly in the microwave or stove to make it easier to spread.
3. Assemble: Spread a small amount of almond butter on each apple slice, or use the almond butter as a dip.
4. Sprinkle with cinnamon: Dust the apple slices with ground cinnamon for added flavor.
5. Optional toppings: Sprinkle chia seeds or hemp seeds on top for a nutritional boost.
6. Serve: Enjoy immediately as a quick snack, or pack it in an airtight container for on-the-go snacking.

CRISPY KALE CHIPS WITH SEA SALT

PREP TIME
10 minutes

CHILL TIME
15-20 minutes

SERVING SIZE
4 servings

YIELD
....

NUTRITIONAL VALUE

- Calories: 70 | Protein: 2g
- Carbohydrates: 6g | Fat: 5g
- Fiber: 2g | Net Carbs: 4g

INGREDIENT

- 1 large bunch of kale, washed and thoroughly dried
- 1-2 tablespoons olive oil
- ½ teaspoon sea salt (or to taste)
- ¼ teaspoon garlic powder or smoked paprika (optional, for added flavor)

EQUIPMENT NEEDED:

- Baking sheet
- Parchment paper
- Large mixing bowl

TIPS

Even cooking: Rotate the baking sheet halfway through baking to ensure even crisping.
Flavor variations: Try adding nutritional yeast for a cheesy flavor or cayenne pepper for a spicy kick.

INSTRUCTIONS

1. Preheat the oven to 300°F (150°C)
2. Prepare the kale: Remove the thick stems from the kale leaves and tear the leaves into bite-sized pieces.
3. Coat the kale: In a large mixing bowl, toss the kale with olive oil, ensuring each piece is lightly coated. Sprinkle with sea salt and any additional seasonings, like garlic powder
4. Arrange on a baking sheet: Spread the kale pieces in a single layer on the prepared baking sheet. Avoid overcrowding, as this will prevent the kale from becoming crispy.
5. Bake: Place the baking sheet in the oven and bake for 15-20 minutes, or until the kale is crisp and lightly browned. Keep an eye on them after 10 minutes to avoid burning.
6. Cool and serve: Let the kale chips cool for a few minutes before serving. Enjoy immediately or store in an airtight container for up to 2 days.

CUCUMBER ROUNDS WITH HUMMUS AND PAPRIKA

PREP TIME
5 minutes

CHILL TIME
....

SERVING SIZE
4 servings

YIELD
....

NUTRITIONAL VALUE

- Calories: 100 | Protein: 3g
- Carbohydrates: 11g | Fat: 5g
- Fiber: 4g | Net Carbs: 7g

INGREDIENT

- 1 medium cucumber
- ¼ cup hummus (store-bought or homemade)
- ¼ teaspoon paprika (sweet or smoked)
- Fresh herbs for garnish (optional, such as parsley or cilantro)

EQUIPMENT NEEDED:

- Knife and cutting board
- Small spoon

TIPS

Hummus flavors: Try different flavored hummus varieties like roasted red pepper or garlic to mix things up.
Make ahead: Prepare the cucumber rounds ahead of time, but wait to add the hummus until just before serving to keep them fresh and crisp.

INSTRUCTIONS

1. Slice the cucumber: Wash the cucumber and slice it into thick rounds, about ¼-inch thick.
2. Add hummus: Using a small spoon, dollop a bit of hummus onto each cucumber slice.
3. Sprinkle paprika: Lightly sprinkle paprika over each hummus-topped cucumber round for a pop of color and flavor.
4. Optional garnish: For added freshness, top each piece with a small leaf of parsley or cilantro.
5. Serve: Enjoy immediately as a refreshing and satisfying snack

SPICED ROASTED ALMONDS WITH TURMERIC AND BLACK PEPPER

PREP TIME
5 minutes

COOK TIME
15-20 minutes

SERVING SIZE
4 servings

YIELD
......

NUTRITIONAL VALUE
- Calories: 180 | Protein: 6g
- Carbohydrates: 7g | Fat: 15g
- Fiber: 4g | Net Carbs: 3g

INGREDIENT

- 2 cups raw almonds
- 1 tablespoon olive oil
- 1 teaspoon ground turmeric
- ½ teaspoon black pepper
- ½ teaspoon sea salt (or to taste)
- ¼ teaspoon garlic powder (optional)

EQUIPMENT NEEDED:

- Baking sheet
- Parchment paper
- Mixing bowl
- Spoon or spatula

TIPS

Add more spice: For an extra kick, add cayenne pepper or chili powder to the spice mix.
Flavor variations: Try other spices like cumin or paprika for different flavor profiles.

INSTRUCTIONS

1. Preheat the oven: Preheat your oven to 350°F (175°C) and line a baking sheet with parchment paper.

2. Prepare the almond mixture: In a mixing bowl, combine the raw almonds, olive oil, turmeric, black pepper, sea salt, and garlic powder (if using). Toss until the almonds are evenly coated.

3. Spread on a baking sheet: Spread the seasoned almonds in a single layer on the prepared baking sheet.

4. Roast the almonds: Place the baking sheet in the oven and roast for 15-20 minutes, stirring halfway through, until the almonds are golden brown and fragrant. Keep a close eye on them to prevent burning.

5. Cool and serve: Remove the almonds from the oven and let them cool completely before serving

HOMEMADE WHOLE-GRAIN CRACKERS WITH ROSEMARY

PREP TIME
5 minutes

COOK TIME
20-25 minutes

SERVING SIZE
4 servings

YIELD
......

NUTRITIONAL VALUE
- Calories: 120 | Protein: 3g
- Carbohydrates: 15g | Fat: 6g
- Fiber: 2g | Net Carbs: 12g

INGREDIENT

- 1 cup whole-wheat flour
- 1 cup rolled oats
- 1 teaspoon dried rosemary (or 1 tablespoon fresh rosemary, finely chopped)
- ½ teaspoon sea salt
- 1/3 cup olive oil
- ½ cup water (adjust as needed)
- 1 tablespoon sesame seeds (optional)

EQUIPMENT NEEDED:

- Mixing bowl
- Airtight container (for storage)

TIPS

Add flavors: Feel free to experiment with different herbs and spices, like thyme or garlic powder, for varied flavors.
Thickness: For thicker crackers, reduce the baking time slightly.

INSTRUCTIONS

1. Preheat the oven: Preheat your oven to 350°F (175°C) and line a baking sheet with parchment paper.
2. Mix dry ingredients: In a large mixing bowl, combine the whole-wheat flour, rolled oats, dried rosemary, sea salt, and sesame seeds
3. Add wet ingredients: Pour in the olive oil and water. Stir until a dough forms.
4. Roll out the dough: Transfer the dough to a lightly floured surface. Roll it out to about 1/8 inch thick
5. Use a sharp knife or pizza cutter to cut the rolled dough into squares or rectangles.
6. Bake: Bake in the preheated oven for 20-25 minutes, or until the edges are golden brown. Keep an eye on them to avoid burning.
7. Cool and serve: Remove the crackers from the oven and let them cool completely before serving.

QUINOA ENERGY BALLS WITH DATES AND COCOA

PREP TIME
5 minutes

COOK TIME
0 minutes (refrigeration time may vary)

SERVING SIZE
4 servings

YIELD
12 energy balls

NUTRITIONAL VALUE

- Calories: 80 | Protein: 2g
- Carbohydrates: 10g | Fat: 4g
- Fiber: 2g | Net Carbs: 7g

INGREDIENT

- 1 cup cooked quinoa (cooled)
- 1 cup pitted dates, chopped
- ¼ cup unsweetened cocoa powder
- ¼ cup nut butter (such as almond or peanut butter)
- 1 tablespoon maple syrup (optional, for sweetness)
- ¼ teaspoon sea salt
- ¼ cup mini dark chocolate chips (optional

TIPS

Customizable: Add in other mix-ins like chia seeds, flax seeds, or shredded coconut for added nutrition.
Sweetness: Adjust the sweetness by adding more or fewer dates based on your preference.

INSTRUCTIONS

1. Combine ingredients: In a mixing bowl, combine the cooked quinoa, chopped dates, cocoa powder, nut butter, maple syrup (if using), and sea salt. Mix well until fully combined. You can use a food processor for a smoother texture.
2. Fold in chocolate chips: If using, fold in the mini dark chocolate chips for added sweetness and texture.
3. Form the balls: Using your hands, take a small amount of the mixture and roll it into a ball, about 1 inch in diameter. Repeat until all the mixture is used.
4. Chill: Place the energy balls on a baking sheet or plate and refrigerate for at least 30 minutes to firm up.
5. Serve and store: Enjoy the energy balls as a nutritious snack. Store any leftovers in an airtight container in the refrigerator for up to a week.

AVOCADO TOAST ON WHOLE-GRAIN BREAD WITH RADISH AND MICROGREENS

PREP TIME
5 minutes

COOK TIME
0 minutes

SERVING SIZE
2 servings

YIELD
......

NUTRITIONAL VALUE
- Calories: 250 | Protein: 6g
- Carbohydrates: 30g | Fat: 13g
- Fiber: 9g | Net Carbs: 21g

INGREDIENT

- 2 slices whole-grain bread
- 1 ripe avocado
- 1 small radish, thinly sliced
- ¼ cup microgreens (such as arugula or sunflower)
- 1 tablespoon lemon juice
- Salt and pepper to taste
- Red pepper flakes (optional, for heat)

EQUIPMENT NEEDED:

- Toaster or oven
- Fork | Serving plate

TIPS

Variations: Try adding other toppings such as cherry tomatoes, feta cheese, or poached eggs for added flavor and nutrition.
Storage: If you have leftover avocado mash, store it in an airtight container with a little lemon juice on top

INSTRUCTIONS

1. Toast the bread: Toast the whole-grain bread slices in a toaster or oven until golden brown and crispy.
2. Prepare the avocado: In a small bowl, scoop the flesh of the avocado and mash it with a fork. Add lemon juice, salt, and pepper to taste. Mix until well combined.
3. Assemble the toast: Spread the mashed avocado evenly over each slice of toasted bread.
4. Top with radish: Arrange the thinly sliced radish on top of the avocado layer.
5. Add microgreens: Pile the microgreens on top of the radish slices for a fresh, vibrant touch.
6. Season and serve: Sprinkle with additional salt, pepper, and red pepper flakes if desired. Serve immediately and enjoy!

VEGETABLE CRUDITÉS WITH GREEN GODDESS DIP

PREP TIME
10 minutes

COOK TIME
0 minutes

SERVING SIZE
2 servings

YIELD
......

NUTRITIONAL VALUE
- Calories: 150 | Protein: 5g
- Carbohydrates: 12g | Fat: 10g
- Fiber: 3g | Net Carbs: 9g

INGREDIENT

For the Crudités:
- 1 cup baby carrots
- 1 cup cucumber, sliced into sticks
- 1 cup bell peppers (red, yellow, or green), sliced into strips
- 1 cup cherry tomatoes
- 1 cup celery sticks

For the Green Goddess Dip:
- ½ cup Greek yogurt (or dairy-free yogurt)
- ¼ cup mayonnaise (or vegan mayo)
- 1 tablespoon lemon juice
- 1 clove garlic, minced
- 2 tablespoons fresh parsley, chopped
- 2 tablespoons fresh chives, chopped
- 2 tablespoons fresh basil, chopped
- Salt and pepper to taste

INSTRUCTIONS

1. Prepare the vegetables: Wash and cut the baby carrots, cucumber, bell peppers, cherry tomatoes, and celery into bite-sized pieces. Arrange them on a serving platter.
2. Make the dip: In a food processor or blender, combine the Greek yogurt, mayonnaise, lemon juice, minced garlic, parsley, chives, and basil. Blend until smooth and creamy.
3. Season the dip: Taste the dip and season with salt and pepper to your preference. Blend again briefly to combine.
4. Serve: Transfer the green goddess dip to a small bowl and place it in the center of the vegetable platter. Serve immediately and enjoy!

Chapter 8

HIGH PROTEIN HIGH FIBER RECIPES

DESSERTS

BERRY CHIA SEED PUDDING

PREP TIME
10 minutes

COOK TIME
0 minutes (requires chilling)

SERVING SIZE
2 servings

YIELD
......

NUTRITIONAL VALUE
- Calories: 180 | Protein: 5g
- Carbohydrates: 25g | Fat: 8g
- Fiber: 12g | Net Carbs: 13g

INGREDIENT

- ½ cup chia seeds
- 2 cups almond milk (or any non-dairy milk)
- 2 tablespoons maple syrup or honey
- 1 teaspoon vanilla extract
- 1 cup mixed berries (fresh or frozen, such as strawberries, blueberries, and raspberries)
- Optional toppings: sliced almonds, coconut flakes, or additional berries

EQUIPMENT NEEDED:

- Mixing bowl | Whisk or spoon
- Serving glasses or bowls
- Refrigerator

TIPS

Apple Variations: Experiment with different apple varieties for varying sweetness and tartness.

INSTRUCTIONS

1. Combine ingredients: In a mixing bowl, whisk together the chia seeds, almond milk, maple syrup (or honey), and vanilla extract until well combined.
2. Let it sit: Allow the mixture to sit for about 10 minutes, then whisk again to prevent clumping.
3. Chill: Cover the bowl and refrigerate for at least 2 hours or overnight to allow the chia seeds to absorb the liquid and thicken.
4. Prepare the berries: If using fresh berries, rinse and slice them. If using frozen, allow them to thaw.
5. Serve: Once the pudding has thickened, give it a good stir. Divide it into serving glasses or bowls and top with mixed berries.
6. Enjoy: Add optional toppings like sliced almonds or coconut flakes for extra crunch!

GRILLED PEACHES WITH HONEY AND LAVENDER

 PREP TIME
10 minutes

 COOK TIME
5 minutes

 SERVING SIZE
2 servings

 YIELD
......

NUTRITIONAL VALUE

- Calories: 120 | Protein: 1g
- Carbohydrates: 31g | Fat: 0.5g
- Fiber: 2g | Net Carbs: 29g

INGREDIENT

- 4 ripe peaches, halved and pitted
- 2 tablespoons honey
- 1 teaspoon dried lavender (culinary grade)
- 1 tablespoon lemon juice
- Optional: Greek yogurt or vanilla ice cream for serving

EQUIPMENT NEEDED:

- Grill or grill pan
- Mixing bowl | Brush or spoon
- Serving plates

TIPS

Apple Variations: Experiment with different apple varieties for varying sweetness and tartness.

INSTRUCTIONS

1. Preheat the grill: Preheat your grill or grill pan over medium heat.
2. Prepare the glaze: In a mixing bowl, combine honey, dried lavender, and lemon juice. Stir until well mixed.
3. Brush the peaches: Brush the cut side of each peach half with the honey-lavender mixture.
4. Grill the peaches: Place the peaches cut side down on the grill. Grill for 3-5 minutes, or until they are warm and have grill marks.
5. Serve: Remove from the grill and drizzle with any remaining honey-lavender mixture.
6. Optional topping: Serve warm with a dollop of Greek yogurt or a scoop of vanilla ice cream, if desired

BAKED CINNAMON APPLES WITH WALNUTS

PREP TIME
10 minutes

COOK TIME
30 minutes

SERVING SIZE
2 servings

YIELD
......

NUTRITIONAL VALUE
- Calories: 210 | Protein: 3g
- Carbohydrates: 28g | Fat: 10g
- Fiber: 4g | Net Carbs: 24g

INGREDIENT

- 4 medium apples (such as Granny Smith or Honeycrisp), cored and sliced
- ½ cup walnuts, chopped
- 2 tablespoons honey or maple syrup
- 1 teaspoon ground cinnamon
- ½ teaspoon nutmeg (optional)
- 2 tablespoons unsalted butter or coconut oil, melted
- Optional: Vanilla ice cream or yogurt for serving

EQUIPMENT NEEDED:

- Baking dish
- Mixing bowl
- Spoon or spatula | Oven

TIPS

Apple Variations: Experiment with different apple varieties for varying sweetness and tartness.

INSTRUCTIONS

1. Preheat the oven: Preheat your oven to 350°F (175°C).
2. Prepare the apples: In a mixing bowl, combine the sliced apples, chopped walnuts, honey (or maple syrup), ground cinnamon, nutmeg (if using), and melted butter (or coconut oil). Stir until the apples are well coated.
3. Arrange in baking dish: Transfer the apple mixture into a baking dish, spreading it out evenly.
4. Bake: Bake in the preheated oven for 25-30 minutes, or until the apples are tender and slightly caramelized.
5. Serve: Remove from the oven and let cool slightly. Serve warm, optionally topped with vanilla ice cream or yogurt.
6. Enjoy: Relish the comforting flavors of this healthy dessert!

DARK CHOCOLATE AVOCADO TUFFLES

PREP TIME
10 minutes

COOK TIME
30 minutes

SERVING SIZE
2 servings

YIELD
12 truffles

NUTRITIONAL VALUE
- Calories: 100 | Protein: 1g
- Carbohydrates: 9g | Fat: 7g
- Fiber: 2g | Net Carbs: 7g

INGREDIENT

- 1 ripe avocado, peeled and pitted
- ½ cup dark chocolate chips (at least 70% cocoa)
- 2 tablespoons maple syrup or honey (adjust to taste)
- 1 teaspoon vanilla extract
- Cocoa powder, chopped nuts, or shredded coconut for rolling

EQUIPMENT NEEDED:

- Baking dish
- Mixing bowl
- Spoon or spatula | Oven

TIPS

Flavor variations: Add a pinch of sea salt or a drop of peppermint extract for a different flavor twist.
Serving suggestion: Pair with fresh fruit or a glass of almond milk for a delightful treat.

INSTRUCTIONS

1. Melt the chocolate: In a microwave-safe bowl, melt the dark chocolate chips in 20-second intervals, stirring in between, until smooth.
2. Blend ingredients: In a food processor, combine the melted chocolate, avocado, maple syrup (or honey), and vanilla extract. Blend until creamy and well combined.
3. Taste and adjust: Taste the mixture and add more sweetener if desired, blending again until smooth.
4. Chill the mixture: Transfer the mixture to a bowl and refrigerate for about 30 minutes to firm up.
5. Form the truffles: Once chilled, scoop out tablespoon-sized portions of the mixture and roll them into balls using your hands.
6. Coat the truffles: Roll each truffle in cocoa powder, chopped nuts, or shredded coconut, depending on your preference.

CHOCOLATE COVERED STRAWBERRIES WITH SEA SALT

 PREP TIME
10 minutes

 COOK TIME
30 minutes

 SERVING SIZE
2 servings

 YIELD
12 strawberries

NUTRITIONAL VALUE

- Calories: 60 | Protein: 1g
- Carbohydrates: 8g | Fat: 3g
- Fiber: 1g | Net Carbs: 7g

INGREDIENT

- 12 large fresh strawberries, washed and dried
- 1 cup dark chocolate chips (at least 70% cocoa)
- Sea salt, for sprinkling

EQUIPMENT NEEDED:

- Baking sheet
- Parchment paper
- Microwave-safe bowl
- Fork or toothpick
- Refrigerator

TIPS

Storage: Store any leftovers in the refrigerator for up to 3 days.
Add toppings: For extra flavor, consider drizzling white chocolate over the dark chocolate once set.

INSTRUCTIONS

1. Prepare the baking sheet: Line a baking sheet with parchment paper and set aside.
2. Melt the chocolate: In a microwave-safe bowl, melt the dark chocolate chips in 20-second intervals, stirring in between, until smooth.
3. Dip the strawberries: Hold each strawberry by the stem, dip it into the melted chocolate, and twist to coat evenly. Allow any excess chocolate to drip off.
4. Place on baking sheet: Place the coated strawberries on the prepared baking sheet.
5. Sprinkle with sea salt: While the chocolate is still wet, sprinkle a small pinch of sea salt on each strawberry.
6. Chill: Place the baking sheet in the refrigerator for about 30 minutes, or until the chocolate has hardened.
7. Serve: Enjoy the strawberries chilled as a delightful dessert!

ALMOND FLOUR BANANA BREAD

PREP TIME
10 minutes

COOK TIME
50 minutes

SERVING SIZE
2 servings

YIELD
1 loaf (about 10 slices)

NUTRITIONAL VALUE
- Calories: 150 | Protein: 4g
- Carbohydrates: 12g | Fat: 10g
- Fiber: 2g | Net Carbs: 10g

INGREDIENT

- 3 ripe bananas, mashed
- 3 cups almond flour
- 3 large eggs
- 1/4 cup maple syrup or honey
- 1 teaspoon vanilla extract
- 1 teaspoon baking soda
- 1/2 teaspoon salt
- Optional: 1/2 teaspoon cinnamon, 1/2 cup chopped walnuts or chocolate chips

INSTRUCTIONS

1. Preheat oven to 350°F (175°C) and grease a loaf pan.
2. Mash bananas and mix with eggs, maple syrup, and vanilla.
3. In another bowl, mix almond flour, baking soda, salt, and optional cinnamon.
4. Combine wet and dry ingredients, folding in walnuts or chocolate chips if desired.
5. Pour batter into the pan and smooth the top.
6. Bake for 50-60 minutes until a toothpick comes out clean.
7. Cool in the pan for 10 minutes, then transfer to a wire rack before slicing.

TIPS

Storage: Store in an airtight container for up to 3 days or freeze for longer storage.
Ripeness matters: The riper the bananas, the sweeter and more flavorful the bread

OATMEAL RAISIN COOKIES WITH FLAXSEED

PREP TIME
10 minutes

COOK TIME
12 minutes

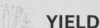
SERVING SIZE
2 servings

YIELD
24 cookies

NUTRITIONAL VALUE
- Calories: 100 | Protein: 2g
- Carbohydrates: 12g | Fat: 5g
- Fiber: 2g | Net Carbs: 9g

INGREDIENT

- 1 cup rolled oats
- 1 cup almond flour
- 1/2 cup coconut sugar or brown sugar
- 1/4 cup ground flaxseed mixed with 1/2 cup water (flax egg)
- 1/2 teaspoon baking soda
- 1/2 teaspoon cinnamon
- 1/4 teaspoon salt
- 1/2 cup raisins
- 1/4 cup coconut oil, melted
- 1 teaspoon vanilla extract

TIPS

Add-ins: Feel free to add chopped nuts or dark chocolate chips for extra flavor. Storage: Store in an airtight container for up to a week.

INSTRUCTIONS

1. Preheat your oven to 350°F (175°C) and line a baking sheet with parchment paper.
2. Make flax egg: In a small bowl, mix the ground flaxseed with water and let it sit for about 5 minutes until it thickens.
3. In a mixing bowl, whisk together the rolled oats, almond flour, coconut sugar, baking soda, cinnamon, and salt.
4. In another bowl, combine the melted coconut oil, flax egg, and vanilla extract. Mix well.
5. Combine wet and dry: Pour the wet mixture into the dry mixture and stir until combined. Fold in the raisins.
6. Using a cookie scoop or spoon, drop spoonfuls of dough onto the prepared baking sheet, spacing them about 2 inches apart.
7. Bake: Bake for 12-15 minutes or until the edges are golden.

BLUEBERRY LEMON ZEST MUFFINS (GLUTEN-FREE)

PREP TIME
10 minutes

COOK TIME
20 minutes

SERVING SIZE
2 servings

YIELD
12 muffins

NUTRITIONAL VALUE
- Calories: 120 | Protein: 4g
- Carbohydrates: 10g | Fat: 8g
- Fiber: 3g | Net Carbs: 7g

INGREDIENT

- 2 cups almond flour
- 1/2 cup coconut flour
- 1/2 cup coconut sugar or honey
- 1 tablespoon baking powder
- 1/2 teaspoon salt
- 3 large eggs
- 1/2 cup unsweetened almond milk
- 1/4 cup coconut oil, melted
- Zest of 1 lemon
- 1 cup fresh or frozen blueberries

TIPS

Add-ins: Add a tablespoon of chia seeds for added texture and nutrition.
Storage: Store in an airtight container for up to 5 days, or freeze for up to a month.

INSTRUCTIONS

1. Preheat the oven: Preheat your oven to 350°F (175°C). Line a muffin tin with silicone or paper liners.
2. Mix dry ingredients: In a large mixing bowl, combine the almond flour, coconut flour, coconut sugar, baking powder, and salt.
3. Mix wet ingredients: In another bowl, whisk together the eggs, almond milk, melted coconut oil, and lemon zest.
4. Combine wet and dry: Pour the wet ingredients into the dry ingredients and stir until just combined. Gently fold in the blueberries.
5. Divide the batter evenly among the muffin cups, filling each about 2/3 full.
6. Bake: Bake for 18-20 minutes, or until a toothpick inserted in the center comes out clean.
7. Cool and serve: Allow the muffins to cool in the tin for 5 minutes before transferring them to a wire rack to cool completely

MANGO TURMERIC NICE CREAM

 PREP TIME
10 minutes

 COOK TIME
0 minutes

 SERVING SIZE
2 servings

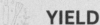 **YIELD**
....

NUTRITIONAL VALUE

- Calories: 180 | Protein: 2g
- Carbohydrates: 45g | Fat: 1g
- Fiber: 5g | Net Carbs: 40g

INGREDIENT

- 2 ripe bananas, sliced and frozen
- 1 cup ripe mango chunks (fresh or frozen)
- 1/2 teaspoon ground turmeric
- 1 tablespoon coconut milk (or any plant-based milk)
- Optional: 1 tablespoon honey or maple syrup for added sweetness

TIPS

Variations: You can add other fruits like pineapple or peaches for different flavor combinations.

Storage: Store any leftovers in the freezer for up to a week; let sit at room temperature for a few minutes before serving to soften.

INSTRUCTIONS

1. Prepare bananas: Ensure the bananas are sliced and frozen. This will give your nice cream a creamy texture.
2. Blend ingredients: In a food processor or high-speed blender, combine the frozen bananas, mango chunks, turmeric, and coconut milk.
3. Process until smooth: Blend until the mixture is smooth and creamy, stopping to scrape down the sides as needed. If the mixture is too thick, add a bit more coconut milk to help it blend.
4. Taste and adjust sweetness: Taste the nice cream. If you prefer it sweeter, add honey or maple syrup and blend again until combined.
5. Scoop the nice cream into bowls and serve immediately for a soft-serve texture.
6. Optional freezing: If you want a firmer texture, transfer the nice cream to an airtight container and freeze for about 1 hour before serving.

GREEK YOGURT BARK WITH BERRIES AND NUTS

PREP TIME
10 minutes

CHILL TIME
2 hours

SERVING SIZE
12 pieces

YIELD
....

NUTRITIONAL VALUE

- Calories: 180 | Protein: 2g
- Carbohydrates: 45g | Fat: 1g
- Fiber: 5g | Net Carbs: 40g

INGREDIENT

- 2 ripe bananas, sliced and frozen
- 1 cup ripe mango chunks (fresh or frozen)
- 1/2 teaspoon ground turmeric
- 1 tablespoon coconut milk (or any plant-based milk)
- Optional: 1 tablespoon honey or maple syrup for added sweetness

TIPS

Variations: You can add other fruits like pineapple or peaches for different flavor combinations.

Storage: Store any leftovers in the freezer for up to a week; let sit at room temperature for a few minutes before serving to soften.

INSTRUCTIONS

1. Prepare bananas: Ensure the bananas are sliced and frozen. This will give your nice cream a creamy texture.
2. Blend ingredients: In a food processor or high-speed blender, combine the frozen bananas, mango chunks, turmeric, and coconut milk.
3. Process until smooth: Blend until the mixture is smooth and creamy, stopping to scrape down the sides as needed. If the mixture is too thick, add a bit more coconut milk to help it blend.
4. Taste and adjust sweetness: Taste the nice cream. If you prefer it sweeter, add honey or maple syrup and blend again until combined.
5. Scoop the nice cream into bowls and serve immediately for a soft-serve texture.
6. Optional freezing: If you want a firmer texture, transfer the nice cream to an airtight container and freeze for about 1 hour before serving.

GREEK YOGURT BARK WITH BERRIES AND NUTS

 PREP TIME
10 minutes

 CHILL TIME
2 hours

 SERVING SIZE
12 pieces

 YIELD
....

NUTRITIONAL VALUE
- Calories: 60 | Protein: 4g
- Carbohydrates: 8g | Fat: 2g
- Fiber: 1g | Net Carbs: 6g

INGREDIENT

- 2 cups plain Greek yogurt (full-fat or low-fat)
- 2 tablespoons honey or maple syrup (to taste)
- 1 cup mixed berries (strawberries, blueberries, raspberries)
- 1/4 cup nuts (almonds, walnuts, or pistachios), chopped
- Optional: 1 teaspoon vanilla extract

TIPS

Customization: Feel free to add other toppings like dark chocolate chips, coconut flakes, or dried fruits for added flavor and texture.

Serving suggestion: Serve as a healthy snack or dessert option, especially during warmer months.

INSTRUCTIONS

1. Prepare the baking sheet: Line a baking sheet with parchment paper, allowing the edges to hang over for easy removal later.
2. Mix yogurt: In a mixing bowl, combine the Greek yogurt, honey (or maple syrup), and vanilla extract, stirring until well combined.
3. Spread the yogurt: Pour the yogurt mixture onto the prepared baking sheet, spreading it into an even layer about 1/4 inch thick.
4. Add toppings: Sprinkle the mixed berries and chopped nuts evenly over the yogurt.
5. Place the baking sheet in the freezer and freeze for at least 2 hours or until completely solid.
6. Slice and serve: Once frozen, remove the yogurt bark from the baking sheet using the parchment paper. Cut it into pieces using a knife or pizza cutter.
7. Store: Store any leftovers in an airtight container in the freezer for up to a month.

CHAPTER 9

Meal Plans and Guidelines

14-Day Meal Plan for Beginners

Week 1

S/N	BREAKFAST	LUNCH	DINNER	SNACKS
1	Golden Turmeric Oatmeal with Berries	Roasted Beet and Walnut Salad (2 cups)	Baked Salmon with Dill and Lemon (1 fillet) with Grilled Asparagus (1 cup)	Crispy Kale Chips (1 cup)
2	Apple Cinnamon Overnight Oats (1 bowl)	Mediterranean Chickpea Salad (2 cups)	Turmeric and Lemon Roasted Chicken (1 thigh) with Quinoa Pilaf (1 cup)	Trail Mix (1/4 cup)
3	Green Goddess Smoothie Bowl (1 bowl)	Farro and Roasted Vegetable Salad (2 cups)	Vegetarian Lentil and Vegetable Curry (1 bowl) with Brown Rice (1/2 cup)	Berry and Chia Seed Pudding (1 cup)
4	Berry Blitz Antioxidant Smoothie (1 glass)	Spinach and Strawberry Salad (2 cups)	Mediterranean Fish Stew (1 bowl) with Whole Grain Bread (1 slice)	Apple Slices with Almond Butter (1 apple)
5	Avocado Toast with Smoked Salmon (1 slice)	Cucumber and Tomato Salad (2 cups)	Herb-Crusted Lamb Chops (2 chops) with Garlic Sautéed Green Beans (1 cup)	Spiced Roasted Almonds (1/4 cup)

14-Day Meal Plan for Beginners

Week 1

S/N	BREAKFAST	LUNCH	DINNER	SNACKS
6	Spinach and Mushroom Egg Muffins (2 muffins)	Three-Bean Salad (2 cups)	Slow Cooker Chicken and Wild Rice Soup (1 bowl)	Cucumber Rounds with Hummus (1 cup)
7	Oatmeal Raisin Cookies with Flaxseed (2 cookies)	Lemony Garlic Hummus with Veggies (1 cup)	Roasted Butternut Squash and Turmeric Soup (1 bowl)	Berry Chia Seed Pudding (1 cup)

14-Day Meal Plan for Beginners

WEEK 2

S/N	BREAKFAST	LUNCH	DINNER	SNACKS
1	Chocolate Covered Strawberries (4 berries)	Quinoa and Berry Salad (2 cups)	Baked Chicken Thighs with Cauliflower Mash (1 thigh)	Vegetable Crudités with Green Goddess Dip (1 cup)
2	Mango Turmeric Nice Cream (1 bowl)	Lentil and Vegetable Curry (1 bowl)	Slow Cooker Grass-Fed Beef Stew (1 bowl)	Almond Flour Crackers with Cream Cheese Dip (1 cup)
3	Blueberry Lemon Zest Muffins (2 muffins)	Roasted Vegetable Quinoa Salad (2 cups)	Baked Salmon with Dill and Lemon (1 fillet) with Roasted Rainbow Carrots (1 cup)	Dark Chocolate Avocado Truffles (1 truffle)
4	Berry Blast Anti-Inflammatory Smoothie (1 glass)	Kale and Apple Salad (2 cups)	Turkey and Vegetable Stir-Fry (1 bowl)	Spiced Roasted Almonds (1/4 cup)
5	Tropical Inflammation Fighter Smoothie (1 glass)	Roasted Portobello Mushroom Steaks (2 steaks)	Vegetarian Stuffed Bell Peppers (1 pepper)	Baked Cinnamon Apples with Walnuts (1 apple)

14-Day Meal Plan for Beginners

Week 2

S/N	BREAKFAST	LUNCH	DINNER	SNACKS
6	Egg and Vegetable Scramble (2 eggs with 1 cup veggies)	Wild Rice and Mushroom Medley (2 cups)	Roasted Brussels Sprouts with Butternut Squash and Cranberries (1 bowl)	Homemade Whole-Grain Crackers (1 cup)
7	Almond Butter and Banana Toast (1 slice)	Mediterranean Chickpea Salad (2 cups)	Spinach and Mushroom Egg Muffins (2 muffins)	Greek Yogurt Bark with Berries (1 piece)

Meal Timing and Portion Sizes

- Breakfast: Aim to have breakfast within an hour of waking up. Portion sizes are typically 1 serving per meal, tailored to individual hunger levels.
- Lunch: Plan for lunch 3-4 hours after breakfast. Aiming for 2 cups of salad or hearty grain dishes is a good way to ensure satiety.
- Dinner: Dinner should be consumed 3-4 hours after lunch, with 1 serving of protein (about the size of your palm) and 1-2 cups of vegetables.
- Snacks: Include 1-2 snacks between meals if needed to manage hunger and maintain energy. Aiming for a portion size of around 1 cup or 1/4 cup for nuts or seeds is recommended.

Additional Tips

- Hydration: Drink plenty of water throughout the day, aiming for at least 8 cups, and consider herbal teas that have anti-inflammatory properties.
- Prep in Advance: Batch cook meals on weekends to save time during busy weekdays.
- Listen to Your Body: Adjust portion sizes based on your hunger levels and physical activity.

CHAPTER 10

Sustaining Your New Lifestyle

Embarking on a journey toward a healthier lifestyle through a high-protein and high-fiber diet is commendable, but sustaining these changes requires commitment and adaptability. It's essential to recognize that achieving long-term health and wellness is not merely about following a meal plan or a specific diet for a limited time. Instead, it's about cultivating habits that integrate seamlessly into your daily life, allowing you to thrive physically, mentally, and emotionally.

The Importance of Sustainable Change

Making sustainable changes means embracing a lifestyle rather than a diet. A successful health journey is built on a foundation of flexibility, balance, and personalization. Rather than adhering rigidly to restrictive diets, focus on incorporating a variety of whole foods that you enjoy and that support your health goals. Sustainable changes also involve:

- Listening to Your Body: Pay attention to hunger cues and learn to differentiate between physical hunger and emotional cravings. This awareness will help you make healthier choices aligned with your body's needs.

- Adapting to Life Changes: Life is full of transitions whether it's a new job, a move, or changes in your family dynamics. Embrace the idea that your dietary needs and routines may evolve, and be open to adjusting your habits accordingly.

Tips for Maintaining Motivation and Commitment

Staying motivated can be one of the biggest challenges when trying to maintain a new lifestyle. Here are some strategies to keep your momentum going:

1. Set Realistic Goals: Break your long-term goals into smaller, achievable milestones. Celebrate your progress along the way, whether it's losing a few pounds, completing a workout, or trying a new recipe.
2. Track Your Progress: Keep a food journal, use an app, or take photos of your meals. Documenting your journey can help you stay accountable and provide insight into what works best for you.
3. Mix It Up: Avoid monotony by experimenting with new recipes, cooking techniques, and foods. Keep your meals interesting to prevent boredom and encourage you to stick with your plan.
4. Create a Routine: Establishing a consistent routine for meal planning, prepping, and exercise can make healthy choices feel more automatic and less burdensome.
5. Focus on the Benefits: Remind yourself of the positive changes you've experienced, whether it's improved energy levels, better mood, or enhanced physical performance. Keeping these benefits in mind can boost your motivation.

Seeking Support and Accountability

The journey to a healthier lifestyle doesn't have to be solitary. Surrounding yourself with a supportive network can significantly enhance your success:

- Engage Friends and Family: Share your goals with loved ones and invite them to join you in your journey. Whether it's cooking meals together, participating in workouts, or simply being there to encourage you, their support can be invaluable.
- Join a Community: Consider joining a local or online support group that aligns with your health goals. Being part of a community can provide motivation, shared experiences, and accountability.
- Work with a Professional: If you feel overwhelmed, consider seeking the guidance of a registered dietitian, nutritionist, or health coach. They can provide tailored advice, resources, and strategies to help you stay on track.

Sustaining your new lifestyle is an ongoing journey that involves continuous learning, adaptation, and self-compassion. Embrace the process, and remember that setbacks are part of the journey. By making sustainable changes, maintaining motivation, and seeking support, you can create a fulfilling and healthy life that brings you joy and vitality.

As you continue to nourish your body and mind, take pride in every step you take toward your goals. With time, patience, and perseverance, you will not only achieve your desired outcomes but also develop a lasting relationship with food and health that will enrich your life for years to come.

Tips for Long-Term Success

Incorporating a high-protein and high-fiber diet into your daily life is a powerful step toward better health and well-being. To ensure that these dietary changes become sustainable and rewarding, consider the following practical tips:

Practical Tips for Daily Incorporation

1. Plan Your Meals: Dedicate time each week to plan your meals and snacks. This proactive approach helps you make healthier choices and minimizes the temptation to grab convenience foods. Use a calendar or meal planning app to map out your meals for the week.
2. Prep in Batches: Cooking in batches can save you time and energy throughout the week. Prepare large portions of high-protein and high-fiber foods, such as grilled chicken, quinoa, or roasted vegetables. Store them in portioned containers for easy access during busy days.
3. Choose High-Quality Ingredients: Invest in fresh, whole foods when grocery shopping. Opt for lean meats, legumes, whole grains, and a variety of fruits and vegetables. Shopping at farmers' markets or local co-ops can help you find high-quality produce while supporting your community.

4. Keep Healthy Snacks on Hand: Stock your pantry and fridge with healthy snacks that are high in protein and fiber. Options like nuts, Greek yogurt, hummus with veggies, or whole grain crackers can help you avoid unhealthy choices when hunger strikes.

5. Experiment with Recipes: Don't be afraid to get creative in the kitchen. Explore new recipes that feature high-protein and high-fiber ingredients. This experimentation can keep your meals exciting and enjoyable.

6. Balance Your Plate: Aim for a balanced plate that includes a protein source, a fiber-rich carbohydrate, and healthy fats. This combination not only enhances satiety but also provides your body with essential nutrients.

Listening to Your Body

One of the most important aspects of maintaining a healthy diet is to listen to your body. Here are some ways to practice mindful eating:

- Tune Into Hunger Signals: Pay attention to your body's hunger and fullness cues. Eat when you're hungry, and stop when you're satisfied. This practice can help you develop a healthier relationship with food.
- Adjust as Needed: Understand that your nutritional needs may change over time. Factors such as age, activity level, stress, and health conditions can affect your dietary requirements. Be open to adjusting your food choices and portion sizes based on how you feel.
- Practice Mindfulness: Incorporate mindfulness techniques into your meals. Focus on the flavors, textures, and aromas of your food. Eating without distractions can enhance your enjoyment and help you recognize when you're full.

Celebrating Success and Staying Positive

Celebrating your successes, no matter how small, is vital for maintaining motivation and a positive mindset. Here's how to cultivate a celebratory approach to your journey:

1. Acknowledge Your Achievements: Take time to reflect on your progress. Celebrate milestones like completing a week of meal prepping, trying a new recipe, or reaching a fitness goal. Recognizing these achievements fosters a sense of accomplishment.

2. Create a Reward System: Set up a reward system for yourself when you reach certain goals. Treat yourself to something enjoyable, like a spa day, a new workout outfit, or a night out with friends.

3. Stay Positive: Cultivate a positive mindset by focusing on what you've gained through your journey rather than what you've given up. Appreciate the energy, health, and vitality that a high-protein and high-fiber diet brings to your life.

4. Connect with Others: Share your successes with friends, family, or online communities. Surrounding yourself with supportive individuals who understand your journey can help you stay.

CHAPTER 11

Practical Tips for Daily Incorporation

1. Plan Your Meals: Dedicate time each week to plan your meals and snacks. This proactive approach helps you make healthier choices and minimizes the temptation to grab convenience foods. Use a calendar or meal planning app to map out your meals for the week.

2. Prep in Batches: Cooking in batches can save you time and energy throughout the week. Prepare large portions of high-protein and high-fiber foods, such as grilled chicken, quinoa, or roasted vegetables. Store them in portioned containers for easy access during busy days.

3. Choose High-Quality Ingredients: Invest in fresh, whole foods when grocery shopping. Opt for lean meats, legumes, whole grains, and a variety of fruits and vegetables. Shopping at farmers' markets or local co-ops can help you find high-quality produce while supporting your community.

4. Keep Healthy Snacks on Hand: Stock your pantry and fridge with healthy snacks that are high in protein and fiber. Options like nuts, Greek yogurt, hummus with veggies, or whole grain crackers can help you avoid unhealthy choices when hunger strikes.

5. Experiment with Recipes: Don't be afraid to get creative in the kitchen. Explore new recipes that feature high-protein and high-fiber ingredients. This experimentation can keep your meals exciting and enjoyable.

6. Balance Your Plate: Aim for a balanced plate that includes a protein source, a fiber-rich carbohydrate, and healthy fats. This combination not only enhances satiety but also provides your body with essential nutrients.

Listening to Your Body

One of the most important aspects of maintaining a healthy diet is to listen to your body. Here are some ways to practice mindful eating:

- Tune Into Hunger Signals: Pay attention to your body's hunger and fullness cues. Eat when you're hungry, and stop when you're satisfied. This practice can help you develop a healthier relationship with food.
- Adjust as Needed: Understand that your nutritional needs may change over time. Factors such as age, activity level, stress, and health conditions can affect your dietary requirements. Be open to adjusting your food choices and portion sizes based on how you feel.
- Practice Mindfulness: Incorporate mindfulness techniques into your meals. Focus on the flavors, textures, and aromas of your food. Eating without distractions can enhance your enjoyment and help you recognize when you're full.

Incorporating a high-protein and high-fiber diet into your life is a transformative journey that goes beyond food choices. By following these practical tips, listening to your body, and celebrating your successes, you can create a lasting and positive relationship with food and health. Embrace the process, stay flexible, and remember that every step you take brings you closer to your goals. With commitment, patience, and a positive attitude, you can achieve long-term success and enjoy the benefits of a healthier lifestyle.

The Advantages of Soluble and Insoluble Fiber for Digestive Health and Well-Being

Fiber is needed for a healthy digestive tract and a variety of other body processes. Let's look at how soluble and insoluble fiber benefit digestive health and beyond.

1. Soluble Fiber Promotes Gut Health and Satiety:
Improves Digestion: Soluble fiber feeds the good bacteria in your gut, helping to maintain a healthy gut microbiota. These bacteria convert fiber into short-chain fatty acids (SCFAs), which reduce inflammation and improve the gut lining.
- Increases Fullness: The gel generated by soluble fiber slows digestion, allowing you to feel fuller for longer after eating. This can help with overall calorie consumption and weight management.
Reduces Digestive Discomfort: Soluble fiber can help control irritable bowel syndrome (IBS) by softening stools and preventing diarrhea.

2. Insoluble fiber promotes colon health and regularity.
- Prevents constipation: Insoluble fiber bulks up the stool, making it easier to move through the intestines. This encourages regular bowel motions and prevents digestive problems such as constipation, hemorrhoids, and diverticulosis.
Promotes Colon Health: By increasing the transit time of food through the digestive tract, insoluble fiber aids in the removal of waste materials and lowers the chance of developing colon-related illnesses.

3. Overall Wellbeing:
In addition to its digestive benefits, fiber can help reduce the risk of a variety of chronic diseases. According to studies, high-fiber diets are associated with a lower risk of heart disease, stroke, type 2 diabetes, and some malignancies, including colon cancer. Fiber-rich diets also aid in weight management by increasing satiety and decreasing overeating.

Fiber's Impact on Blood Sugar and Cholesterol

Fiber is essential for controlling blood sugar levels and lowering cholesterol, both of which are important in preventing chronic illnesses like diabetes and heart disease.

1. Blood Sugar Regulation:
Soluble fiber slows the absorption of sugar in the circulation. By producing a gel in the digestive tract, it slows the digestion and absorption of carbs, resulting in a more gradual release of glucose into the blood. This helps to keep blood sugar levels stable, which is especially important for people who have diabetes or insulin resistance

Key Advantages of Soluble Fiber for Blood Sugar Control:
Improves blood sugar control after meals, lowering the incidence of type 2 diabetes.
increases insulin sensitivity, allowing the body to utilize glucose more efficiently.
assists in the management of diabetes by lowering the frequency and intensity of blood sugar swings.

Increased fiber consumption, particularly from soluble fiber sources such as oats, legumes, and fruits, can dramatically improve blood sugar management in people with or at risk of diabetes.

2. Cholesterol reduction:
Soluble fiber also binds to bile acids in the digestive tract, which are composed of cholesterol. The fiber retains the bile, which is then expelled rather than reabsorbed. In reaction, the liver consumes more cholesterol to generate bile acids, decreasing LDL (bad) cholesterol levels in the bloodstream.

Key Advantages of Fiber for Heart Health:
lowers total and LDL cholesterol levels, lowering the risk of cardiovascular disease.
Promotes healthy blood pressure, which benefits cardiovascular health.
Lowers the risk of atherosclerosis (the accumulation of cholesterol in the arteries) by preventing high cholesterol levels.

Consuming fiber-rich foods, particularly those high in soluble fiber, such as oats and flaxseeds, can help lower cholesterol and promote heart health.

Fiber may be nutrition's unsung hero, but its importance in supporting digestive health, managing blood sugar, and decreasing cholesterol cannot be underestimated. Incorporating a range of soluble and insoluble fiber sources into your diet can provide several health benefits, such as improved digestion, better blood sugar control, and improved heart health. Whether you want to improve your o

Listening to your body is essential on this journey. Everyone's response to food and activity changes is different. Monitor your energy levels, digestion, mood, and any symptoms of inflammation. If you experience prolonged symptoms or pain, be willing to make changes to your diet or exercise program. This could include trying new anti-inflammatory foods, adjusting portion sizes, or experimenting with new types of physical activity. Being adaptable and attentive to your body's cues will allow you to identify the best solution for your specific needs.

Seeking professional counsel and assistance can also be quite valuable as you work through your anti-inflammatory diet. Consult a trained dietitian or nutritionist with expertise in anti-inflammatory foods or chronic illness management. They may offer specialized advice, assist you in creating a customized meal plan, and suggest techniques for overcoming any difficulties that may arise along the road. Participating in support groups or online forums can also help you connect with others who are going through the same thing, providing encouragement, shared experiences, and helpful advice. Remember that adopting an anti-inflammatory lifestyle is a personal journey that involves patience and adaptability, and seeking professional help can improve your chances of reaching long-term health benefits.

Balance carbohydrates and fats

In order to achieve optimal health, it is critical to balance your carbohydrate, fat, and protein intake. These three macronutrients have diverse functions in the body, and knowing how to manage them can help you attain a balanced diet that promotes energy, weight control, and overall well-being. This chapter will look at the importance of macronutrient balance, the many types of carbohydrates and their effects on blood sugar levels, and the critical role healthy fats play in heart health and brain function.

The importance of balancing carbohydrates, fats, and protein in a healthy diet

A balanced and sustainable diet requires a mix of carbohydrates, lipids, and proteins. Each macronutrient plays a distinct role in feeding and sustaining the body's many processes.

Carbohydrates give rapid energy and are the body's principal source of fuel, particularly in the brain and muscles. They are transformed into glucose (sugar), which can be used immediately or stored for future use.

Fats provide a more concentrated source of energy and are essential for brain function, hormone production, and the absorption of fat-soluble vitamins A, D, E, and K. Healthy fats also help maintain cell structure and provide long-term energy.

Proteins are the fundamental components of muscle, skin, enzymes, and other important tissues. They promote muscle healing, immunological function, and general development.

Different Carbohydrates and Their Effect on Blood Sugar Levels

Carbohydrates are an important source of energy, but they are not all made equal. There are two types of carbs: simple carbohydrates and complex carbohydrates, each with a unique influence on blood sugar levels and energy.

1. Simple carbohydrates:
Simple carbohydrates are sugars that are readily absorbed by the body, resulting in high blood glucose levels. They are commonly present in processed foods, sugary snacks, and beverages. Common sources include:
Table sugar.
Candy and baked foods.
Sweetened beverages (soda and fruit juices)
Certain refined grains (like white bread and pastries)

Because simple carbohydrates are quickly digested, they provide a small burst of energy, followed by a "crash" as blood sugar levels decrease, resulting in hunger and cravings shortly after. Consuming too many simple carbohydrates can lead to weight gain and an increased risk of type 2 diabetes.

2. Complex carbohydrates:
Complex carbohydrates are composed of longer chains of sugar molecules that take longer to degrade. This causes a slower, more persistent release of glucose into the bloodstream, resulting in consistent energy and improved blood sugar control. Foods high in complex carbs are frequently high in fiber, vitamins, and minerals, making them a healthier option.

Common Sources of Complex Carbohydrates
Whole grains (brown rice, quinoa, and oatmeal)
Vegetables: sweet potatoes, leafy greens, carrots.
- legumes (beans, lentils, and chickpeas)
Whole fruits (apples, berries, and pear)

Glycemic Index:

The glycemic index is a method for determining how rapidly a carbohydrate-rich food elevates blood sugar levels. Foods with a low GI (such as most complex carbs) generate a gradual rise in blood sugar, whereas high GI foods (simple carbs) cause a rapid jump. Choosing low-GI foods can help control blood sugar levels, lower the risk of insulin resistance, and give more consistent energy throughout the day.

Effect of carbohydrates on blood sugar:

Simple carbohydrates induce quick blood sugar spikes, resulting in energy fluctuations and the potential for insulin resistance over time.

Complex carbohydrates provide moderate increases in blood sugar, promoting consistent energy levels and decreasing hunger sensations.

Choosing complex carbs over simple, refined carbohydrates is critical for maintaining stable blood sugar levels, aiding in weight control, and lowering the chance of acquiring chronic diseases such as diabetes and cardiovascular problems.

Measurement Conversions

WEIGHT CONVERSIONS

S/N	METRIC	STANDARD
1	1 gram (g)	0.035 ounces (oz)
2	10 grams (g)	0.35 ounces (oz)
3	100 grams (g)	3.5 ounces (oz)
4	1 kilogram (kg)	2.2 pounds (lbs)
5	500 grams (g)	1.1 pounds (lbs)
6	1 ton (metric)	2204.6 pounds (lbs)

TEMPERATURE CONVERSIONS

S/N	CELCIUS	STANDARD
1	0 °C	32 °F
2	10 °C	50 °F
3	20 °C	68 °F
4	30 °C	86 °F
5	40 °C	104 °F
6	100 °C	212 °F

VOLUME CONVERSIONS

S/N	METRIC	STANDARD
1	1 milliliter (ml)	0.034 fluid ounces (fl oz)
2	5 milliliters (ml)	1 teaspoon (tsp)
3	15 milliliters (ml)	1 tablespoon (tbsp)
4	100 milliliters (ml)	3.4 fluid ounces (fl oz)
5	1 liter (L)	4.2 cups (c)
6	1 liter (L)	33.8 fluid ounces (fl oz)
7	1 cup (c)	240 milliliters (ml)
8	1 pint (pt)	2 cups (c)
9	1 quart (qt)	4 cups (c)
10	1 gallon (gal)	16 cups (c)

Understanding measurement conversions is essential for cooking, especially when following recipes that may use different units. Below is a comprehensive table of common measurement conversions for weight, volume, and temperature, covering both metric and standard units.

Additional Useful Conversions

1 tablespoon (tbsp) = 3 teaspoons (tsp)
1 cup = 16 tablespoons (tbsp)
1 ounce (oz) = 28.35 grams (g)
1 pound (lbs) = 453.59 grams (g)

Made in the USA
Coppell, TX
06 January 2025

44016408R10063